Quartet

The University of Arkansas Press Award for
Arabic Literature in Translation, 1996

ABOUT THE AWARD

"Education is the best means—
probably the only means—
by which nations can cultivate a degree of objectivity
about each other's behavior and intentions."

—J. WILLIAM FULBRIGHT
(1905–1995)

The University of Arkansas Press Award for Arabic Literature in Translation is a unique feature of the nationally acclaimed King Fahd Middle East Studies Program at the J. William Fulbright College of Arts and Sciences. Yearly since 1993, prizes of $7,500 each for both author and translator are awarded for works in fiction, nonfiction, and poetry, and the winning entries are published by the University of Arkansas Press. For more information on the Arabic translation award, please contact Professor John T. DuVal, Translation Program, Kimpel Hall 333, University of Arkansas, Fayetteville, AR 72701   (501) 575-4301.

POEMS BY
MUHAMMAD AFIFI MATAR

Translated from the Arabic by
FERIAL GHAZOUL & JOHN VERLENDEN

The University of Arkansas Press   Fayetteville 1997

Originally published in 1990 by Riad El-Rayyes Books, London

Translation copyright 1997 by the University of Arkansas Board of Trustees

01 00 99 98 97   5 4 3 2 1

Designed by Alice Gail Carter

⊖ The paper used in this publication meets the minimum requirements
of the American National Standard for Permanence of Paper for Printed
Library Materials   Z39.48-1984.

LIBRARY OF CONGRESS CATALOGING-IN-PUBLICATION DATA

Maṭar, Muḥammad ʿAfīfī.
    [Rubāʿīyat al-farah. English and Arabic]
    Quartet of joy : poems/ by Muhammad Afifi Matar; translated
from the Arabic by Ferial Ghazoul and John Verlenden.
        p. cm.
    Originally published: London : Riad El-Rayyes Books, 1990.
    ISBN 1-55728-487-3 (alk. paper). — ISBN 1-55728-488-1 (pbk. :
alk. paper)
    I. Ghazoul, Ferial Jabouri, 1939– . II. Verlenden, John, 1947– .
III. Title.
PJ7846.A8756R75   1997
892'.716—dc21   97-26841
                            CIP

Acknowledgments

Our deepest appreciation goes to Maggie Awadalla, who helped lay out the Arabic text, and to Anthony Calderbank, who provided the Arabic calligraphy. Thanks go to editor Karen Johnson and designer Gail Carter, who both brought a meticulous, caring spirit to the book's final preparation. We also thank our friends and the anonymous manuscript judge for their valuable comments.

Contents

Arabic Text: Ruba'iyat al-farah

All attempts at poetry translation undertake an almost impossible task, but some poetry is so elusive, condensed, syntactically sophisticated, and rhythmically evocative that attempting to translate it into another language seems like sheer madness. Of this madness we—the translators—partake and confess to. But our madness is not without method. It is based on close collaboration between a scholar of Arabic and English literature, Ferial Ghazoul, and a poet in the target language, John Verlenden. This translation, however, is not merely a version produced by a bilingual expert and then polished by a native-speaking poet. It is the outcome of a lengthy process of search and reflection on the possibilities and limits of transposing an aesthetic experience in one language into another language, of transmitting that most specific of cultural products— poetry—to another culture. This process meant, for both of us, delving into the hermetic universe of the poet, Muhammad Afifi Matar, and learning to distinguish his aesthetic logic and codes, to appreciate his subtle inflections of meaning and intricate modes of allusion. We also learned by trial and error to carry over into another language not only the words but something akin to their original charge and power. Our final version is the outcome of dialectical insights and interlocking efforts, which were facilitated by the work site. As colleagues in the same department (English and comparative literature) in an institution committed to intercultural dialogue—an American University in the Arab Republic of Egypt —teeming with different nationalities, cultures, and orientations, we are constantly involved in cultural translations and comparisons.

The translation started with Ghazoul, the scholar-translator, producing two versions of the original Arabic. One was highly literal, listing more than one option for a word or a phrase, and following word order and layout of the original as much as it is possible to do so in the English idiom. The second version reflected her choice of wording and initial layout. Verlenden, the poet-translator, then composed a third version based on his reading of the two. This third version was then discussed by the two of us, pointing out to each other departures from the original or infelicities in the target language. We checked specific points with Matar himself. Words and images were tossed around, syntax was modified, and layout was refined while we explored the semantic field of the original Arabic words or expressions, their etymologies and varied uses; and this went on from one version to another until our seventh and final version. There is, of course, no definitive translation of any text, but there is this provisional final that we feel ready to share with others.

We tried to reproduce the rich intricacy and the wonderful strangeness of the original, because we strongly feel that readers of Arabic poetry translated into English are not simply looking for more poetry with which they are familiar but are seeking to experience what is different. Accordingly, we did not attempt to domesticate the text or naturalize it in such a way that the readers would sense it was simply another poem in their language. At the same time, we realize that the reader's reception of alternative poetics is dependent on experiencing a verbal pleasure and poetic effect. Our own solution to this paradoxical situation was to adhere closely— closely but not mindlessly—to the original wording and imagery and take guarded license with the poem's layout on the page. The original figuration of the poem on the page responds to visual conventions and auditory sensibility of Arab readers. The free running lines of unequal length on the page of the original are themselves a visual marker of modern verse since classical Arabic poetry with its monorhymes and hemistiches looks rigidly symmetrical on the page. We adjusted this given asymmetricality in such a way as to indicate the flow of imagery and the sudden shifts in scenes, as well as to mark the interior monologues and the dramatic dialogues present in the original. Furthermore, Matar, in his endeavor to create poetry that speaks the language of the age but also relates intimately to the language of the tribe, interweaves in the body of his poems classical Arabic verse, Koranic citations, and Sufi aphorisms. We indicate such embedments in the poetic discourse through changes in the layout, signaling visually the difference in registers.

Quartet of Joy (Ruba'iyat al-farah), as well as most of Matar's poetry, is considered difficult, ambiguous, and hermetic. Matar is known as the poet of poets, appealing to connoisseur readers rather than the general Arab public with its taste for declamatory platform poetry. Part of the difficulty in reading Matar lies in the overwhelming richness of his diction, the complexity of his allusions, and the convolution of his syntax. To add to the defamiliarizing effect of the above, printing conventions in Arabic do without vocalization *(tashkil)*—which amounts to leaving the vowels *(harakat)* out of the written text. Because the words lack inflections, they can be misread on the most basic level of intended meaning, and also on the levels of gender and grammatical position. The poetry of Matar, therefore, has its full effect when it is articulated aloud: vocalization, stresses, and caesuras clarify areas that seem obscure or undecidable in silent reading. This does not dismiss the fact that Matar's poetry thrives on polysemy and ambiguity; however, its thrusts become more pointed when properly read, just as, when it is properly experienced and contemplated, its labyrinthine structure reveals a geometry of finesse.

To chart one's way in Matar's poetic discourse, one has to grasp the poet's maneuvers. He charges certain words (such as "lineage," "door," "bird") with specific connotations and thus turns them into poetic building blocks with which he constructs his imaginative universe. His visionary poetry revolves around the homeland, the beloved, and poetry—metonyms of freedom, harmony, and beauty —but these three circles overlap and dissolve into each other; earth and woman become one; poetry and homeland seem faces of the same coin—and the reader is at times unable to tell whether the addressee is the beloved woman or the beloved land. This meshing is part of the poetic strategy of Matar: to demolish the barriers between the metaphoric and the literal. He is also aware of the ambivalent directions a phenomenon may take. Power, passion, and words can lead to despotism, indulgence, and empty chatter or alternately to liberation, fulfilment, and poetry. Only an attentive reading can decipher which aspect of the phenomenon he is referring to. Above all, Matar bewilders and enchants through the technique of image within image, where one metaphor is embedded inside another, and in turn this metaphor is embedded within another, and so on in an escalating vertigo. This *mise-en-abyme*, so typical of the *Arabian Nights*, is transformed in Matar's hand into a dizzying poetics. These images, however, reflect each other, and beneath the forest of imagery there is a rigorous order derived from those absent-present texts, those subtexts of myths, legends, and history—alluded to—which can unravel the entanglement and show the significance of this poetic arabesque.

We have chosen to leave a few Arabic words transliterated (with the minimum of diacritical marks) rather than translated, because they are so culturally specific that a "translation" will only disfigure them. These words, pertaining mainly to Bedouin material culture, Egyptian lore, or Islamic rituals, are italicized in the body of the text, and a glossary at the end explains the meaning and uses of these foreign words, as well as those of other English words derived from Arabic and used in the translation. Intertextual references, allusions, and explications are provided in explanatory notes. The original text of *Quartet of Joy* in Arabic is provided in the back of the book for the benefit of bilingual readers.

Earth Joy

FIRST PRELUDE

The fired shot of glassy water
with translucent bullet:
the sea aimed it—between resting
    and rising up—
and it felled me with rapturous blow;
I blanked out from the glare
    of high-distancing noon . . .

My limbs: a mare.
The sea: a spring season
        of flesh well toned,
spreading for me its tables of hunger,
    dish after dish.
And my dreams: wild birds,
    night surprised them with bafflement
        and the call of space.

Forty doors are the sundial
    of your body
    opened to springs of food and drink:
        I ate and drank.
I monitored my feet,
    saw a step,
    did not however see the way.
Forty doors . . .
    number of the years
    from which I came,
    wearing flesh and blood,
I talk yet am not born.

Sun of midnight and moon of high noon:
is this the melding of homeland
              and exile,
of language with the terror of caverns?

Is it the hour of lengthening shadows,
or the date of watersprings' inner nature,
              bursting out,
         so my body may find completion
         and break into rhymed *fasilas*
              and rhythm-beads?
I say, I who am born of forty women:
         this is the valor of waiting
         and the stumblings of slow greenness.

SECOND PRELUDE

Forty doors . . .
         circles looping out upon circles
         and corridors meshing,
and the trees of stairs branch up
                   and down . . .

My friend Zeno of Elea surprises me
by showing me the space between the arrow
              and the horizon
and fills the void of paper
with the savagery of the race
         between me and the tortoise of beginning
                   and the word of revelation.

And my friend al-Niffari surprises me
with the rose of crimson water
and the glare of sea
and taste of salt air . . .
I end up craving bread,
         and wait for time

and the childhood
of evening talk
and the disclosure
and the moment that stuns.
I who am born of forty women,
I look out for the ravings of memory
and the defiance of forms,
for the earth is arched over
the harvests of death
and the decanters of aged thirst.

Are you, O tavern keeper,
ready to deflower the clay seals,
set the table with goblets,
hunks of food,
bushel baskets of salted grass
and olive?
Or are you turning around
like the head when it drops
from the tree of the body?
And are you—between what
has been and what will be—
a ruler of the space between your first step
on the pebbles of death
and your first step
on the shattering threshhold?
Here is the river squatting,
untying the straps of its sandals
braided from marsh hemp
and softness of grass,
its cloak crisp like hay and braids
of wheat ears,
embroidered by safflower and buttercup;
from its loops hang bands of mulberry
and buds of pomegranate dropping
from the rose of annual blood.
Here is the river changing itself
into a vegetal being teeming with bodies,
with water moss, lotus, the foam of verdure,
and odor of death.

Night is dripping from the tips
          of hands;
between fingers stones cling,
making homes with closed windows
          and unknown corridors.

Are you
          a woman because kings jostle
          between your gown
          and your body's undulations?
Or do kings besiege you
          because you are womanly?
Or are you a woman because your breasts
and thighs are stalls for the trees
          inscribed on the palms of night and day
          and on wind eddies?

Night revealed your legs
          and morn's column stood erect;
between your breasts the earth is stretched
          until the day of Promise!
This is the marriage of elements.
Your shelter of kindling and dry trees
          falls from you,
                    and the horizon's tree rises up.
The wild bees construct their hexagons
          in the courtyard of your ripe *omphalos,*
          proceeding round you as wind
          proceeds row by row,
as if birds were on their heads.
Such is the time of joy and death,
and you are from everything a source
          shaking with fever
          and a cry fluttering
                    in its own blood.
Such is the sign of the will to anger
and the resurrection of the seventh earth.

So look:
      here is the sun picked
      up from its buds
            sprinkling fuzz from its velvet
            on the mound of birth.
You write the *alif* **ا** : a step
      dropping like a shell on the flesh
            of surrendering paper.
You write the *ya'* **ي** : a bed
      quivering in the quicksilver
      of language.
You learn numbers and arithmetic:
      this is one **١** : wrapped
      in singularity,
      widespread and plentiful.
      You draw four **٤** : a house
      with two floors
      open to wind and rain.
You add
      so creatures are pregnant
      in the ceremony of marriage.
You subtract
      so day is stripped from night,
      the date-stone split,
      and the living brought forth
            from the dead.
You divide
      so baskets fill with fish
            and loaves.
You stand on the threshold of colors
      and on temptations of planes.
The pens are trees chopped
      from the rainbow,
      inhabited by sleep,
      mad with images
      where birds of dream and desire nest.
You progress a step toward the hall of forms,
      toward the arcades of the phrase,
            and everything metamorphoses,
            everything metamorphoses . . .

THIRD PRELUDE

Did you say the earth is closer than my blood,
that the bubbling blood is silt from its maps
and fired brick oozing with ancient lineages
    and the mortal remains in ruins?
Did you say argil and potter's clay
    are but rushing and enduring tears?

I said the country is close at hand,
no sooner the sun passes by me,
no sooner the wind throws off the cloak
    of merciful cloud
than I become cracks of colors
    in the twilight of auroral pourings
    and the rhythms of the rains.
Thrusts of sleep into vision
    and night of creation
    into morn of first nebula
    are naught but my steps
    seeking the country
    within the country.

I said the country is close at hand . . .
and my hands are channels of pure touch,
    oozing out over the creatures
    of the kingdom situated between
        the desire-pollen
        flaming with massive rain . . .
        for the wind is pregnant
        and the colored blood
        fused into lineages and progenies
        matches the throb of holy soil
           and the bursting out
        of earth with generation,
        between the water and the dried-up root.

The earth loosened its shadow
worn out by menses, creation, desire,
and my hands are channels
of pure touch . . .
ten fountains of senses.

This is the belly relaxed into domes
seized by naught but the fever of my hands.
The wind, rhythm of the visit;
the steps, from the searing
of my breath.
The mad blazes are tenderness
in an ear of wheat,
roughness
in the slopes of meadows,
and vales are the mad blazes;
and I stretch my hands;
between us lie sea, desert
and mad blazes.

The earth is closer than my blood . . .
for I am earth's elect,
and earth, my own.
The covenants concluded in the Unknown
disseminating progeny in the loins,
the spindle of orbs and fluttering dawn
beneath the throne of God
attest that the pronouncement
of the Adamic covenant
is sealed with the tattoo
of my blood and clay;
the pronouncement attests
that the parchment
of the pledge contracted
between me and God
opens my ribs in
his guarded tablet . . .

So speak up, O my Certitude,
and blow my blood in the Trumpet.
Let my right hand attest that cities
of the living and the dead
under the pure touch quiver,
stirring the eruption of the daily scene
        with apocalyptic vision.

SOME TIME BEFORE SOME DEATH

Is the cloak loosened for the wind?
Or for the sun's face is the powdered dust
        of dawn's copper on your forehead?

Your mare started up neighing in snorts,
        its echo: the clouds and the light shade
        over stretches of earth and deserts.
You rise above the sunstep rising,
        as if the mare is colliding with the spur
        of space;
as you mount its graceful back
the stirrups reach morning's last star.
No newborn sun in dawn's swaddles
can reflect the sparkle of its henna
in the lock of your loose hair.

Touched by the hooves . . .
        next to it the glitter of the stirrups
        reaching the last morning star.
No departing night in planes of dawn
        can meet you running in its old steppes:
a thousand years and the forenoon
        and the night
                transmuting your face,
you neither flare nor melt,
        nor sleep nor wake up;
while you exist in the millenium

of sleeping insomnia,
you do not hear except the earth bleeding,
        showering thunder-spears.
You do not hear nor see
        except the lineage-dust
        of sleeping insomnia
        strewn by the storming sand-wind
as you tie the knot of smoldering revenge
and suffer flames of recollection and yearning.

So, is this youthful wind
                for the unfastened cloak?
Or is the powdered dust of dawn's copper
                for your face?

A thousand years were a thousand doors
sending forth torrents and floods
sweeping off all seedling life
expected from time's womb.
A thousand doors:
        horizons unstitching
                on defeat and ruin.
With your bone you polish the silver fetters,
hoping the fetter-stuff is that of snaffle
        and stirrups,
but women rendered you
                senseless with passion;
they—vestiges of circular seductions
in the dry snuffling of exile;
        a column-like beauty
        materialized before you
        in the furnace of high noon
        when you were lurching
        between arid presence
                and fertile absence;
        she came forward,
        and behind both of you
        vaults of the ancient kings lit up
        with raptures rising
                from the blooming rock.

I said to myself:
  Your secret deluge is over,
  one of your former shreds
   has sought you out,
  a white dove providing
  from the fruits of your chaos,
  from the submersions of *qasidas*
  in muds of creativity and inspiration,
   a budding branch . . .

I said to myself:
  Follow her capricious dance,
  scatter what's left of tears or ashes
  in the forenoon's temptations,
  or the lures of her neighing gutturals,
   or the excitement of her trilled *r*'s . . .

  Follow the hall of the ancient kings
  to man's first fascination with the world
  and the image of what appeared
  in flames of passion for the earth's expanse
  and the skies with lit domes.

I said to myself:
  Follow the gazelle dance,
  she stirs in your blood the craving
  for earth-shaking poetry
  and the hard-to-bear yearning . . .

You don't know if the prey tempts you
  or if she's the hunter watching;

in a moment of man's merciful oblivion
  she screens herself with transparencies
  and sways while your blood
   gushes along.

I said to myself:
Follow her . . .
            and in the hall of kings the ashen magic
            will tie in the remote vaults the knot
                    of secret joy.
    She will be enraptured,
    enraptured I will be,
            and we shall end
                    at the beginning . . .

The touch of palms over coldness of stone
was covenant to melt into its scenes,
abundant life fragmented unto murals:
the taste of river-trickles from grape clusters,
birds in glorious flocks in forests,
blossoms and colored fish in marshes,
slender oars beating rhythm for the *mawwal*
        and the winged dance,
creatures in the nuptials of birds and beasts
        breeding,
soldiers wearing the grace of lofty death;
        and the triumphal arch:
            farmers, wine pressers, fishermen, carvers,
            the king, too, reclining on royal couch,
            handing the queen drinks,
                    she handing him drinks . . .
            the hawk gliding with gold wing,
            the glitter of its eye: a sun
                    illuminating
                            the petrified scene . . .

The old craving for poetry was craning:
your ashes were inundated,
you broke into *qasida*
        contained in petrified chains.
Your limbs wheeled and the calling muttered
        in every limb;

I wheeled and said to myself:
>The mirage breaks forth into water abundant
>with scented breeze and sweet basil
>coming up from shreds of death and ruined remnants,
>your *mawwal* chained in the millenium
>>of sleeping insomnia . . .

The stone trembles, life repeats its course:
>the morning cries of birds and beasts
>>rise up,
>the blossoms open for swarms of butterflies
>and worker bees,
>the *shadoofs* moisten,
>water flows with lotus and colored fish,
>boats are heavy with first fruit,
>soldiers are stationed at frontier towns
>of the country
>>and of lofty death;
>the earth celebrates a wedding,
>the triumphal arch is gnarled
>>with ornamentation,
>and the ancient kings
>>on couches at the moment of coronation . . .

A wind of enchanting opulence . . .
>too long has been your exile,
>>and my exile,
>in the decays of earth and soul.
Wake up from your shreds,
raise from yourself the *qasida*
in the ashes of the heart
about to moisten its bones;
the rhythm in the oars' beat begins:
>flutter so we can be moved
>to the center of the people;
>and the water blast and the ancient sun
>over the king's ruins.
>Keep raising the dream

squandered among the ashes of love,
break free against me
so we flow in life together,
spilling over from rock madness . . .

The sun was turning
in the horizon of high forenoon,
inclining toward absence;

I said to myself:
Forenoon and night transmute your face,
so go chase down the gazelle
delving in her barren playgrounds.

I said to myself:
Start the chase now and leave for this rock
its delayed hour,
hoping that she has hastened
with the delayed love . . .

The silence of the night was knotted
into a country in the vast expanse,
illuminated by wounds,
contracted by windchill seeking cover
in the silence of wounded legends
                and *mawwals,*
and in the damp sleep of the *rabab* wood,
until I woke up and said:
From what places
—when places are wanting in lovers—
have you come?
From what plans recently fled,
becoming free of chains,
to tempt the bygones, the runaways
from the *qasidas* and the love-wait?

She said: You . . . hold back the images
                of the hard-to-bear madness . . .

I tempted the mask from the visage,
        the visage away from the set dates
        squandered among ashes of love;

her hands reached with hesitating tenderness . . .
        the night and the desert expand,
the fugitive river in the bowers of its soil,
winds with braids dew-moist,
and the She-cosmos is dripping *qasidas*
        from her fingers into stars,
drawing closer the primal stirrings
                of beginning's anguish
                provoked by poetry . . .

In your silk, loops were opening:
pollen exuding lodged scents and infatuated butterflies . . .

        two stars on two dunes,
                the softening of the warmed-up wave,
                        two marble columns of desire-sands,
                                two dimples lit by two roses:

a body gathered of fragments
from every past enchantress?
Or is this the state of cosmic blooming
at the instant of Genesis and Creation?

Her apprehensive tenderness hesitated.
I hastened to meet the tenderness
with the flow of receptive tears
shimmering in the cloud of poetry
beckoning the *qasida*;
I said to myself:
        The noble stallions possess
        the recklessness of clouds
        and the impulse for sudden dancing
        in the planes of the earth
        with unfettered language
        and the ringing desire moans
        in the neigh and the book.

I said:

    Look at the clouds . . .
    be the mare of the realm
    as it forms the intimate language
    in your tongue
    and endow my language
    melting in it,
    the distilled language
    of the tribe
       and the neigh . . .

You were heaving with the *qasida*
    contained in sewn-up masses
    of clouds, not yet unstitched . . .

The mirage will not gush forth
except by flashes of her crystalline eyes
and her poor nod to midnight;
    she was calling back her ashes,
    returning her course to dispersed
       elements;
from your hands she slipped away:
toward sand the two dunes flow off
    which glowed in your hands
    as promised in the breasts' full pledge
       to nurture.
In league with the sea's roar
    her wave knotted at her navel,
      her curving mound opening for birth;
at one with the wind and the tatterings
    of clouds is her silk;
as for smashing and precipice,
    her marble falls to each side;

and amidst the rubble heap
the sand-wind of recollection was blowing:
here they slide down out of every slope,
with all manner of brandished swords
    and lances;
      they encircled you,

you didn't know if this was chase's end
or the earth-moving breakthrough
discovering the snare
of timed love!

You slipped off . . .
while the last morning star was all alone
on the horizon,
your mare started up neighing in ancient poetry;
the snaffle loosened in the flash of dream,
and from the stirrups the silver clamp appeared;
this is the destined journey . . .
no time set for it
nor land
save that rising hard-to-bear pain
and the bloody calls afflicting you,
the last of this chaos and the first
from the lineage to rise up:
the eagle besieged.

You used to open up your wounds
whenever that unavenged blood flared
and the arrows of hunting snarled
in the horizons
and the instinct for carnage blazed
in the hands of invaders;
the wounds opened up for the harvest
of what would drop from fallen prey,
and the airs were free
from violent agility
and wind possession,
eagle after eagle . . .

Here is the last eagle besieged
between filigreed summits and clouds;
the earth, with the hard-to-bear pain
and the bleeding of earth-moving cries,
recall the memories of labor pains . . .

Your mare starts up neighing in ancient love
captured in the *qaṣida*.
   You rise above the rising sunstep . . .
   touched by the hooves . . .
   next to it the glitter of the stirrups
     reaching the morning star.
   No given time.
Neither face of high forenoon
nor wily night are subjects of your vision-spilling face;
yours—the realm,
   the decorated throne, the *qasidas*,
   from infusion of the lineage
   of the ashen eagle in your blood,
   and the hard-to-bear cries.

Drums rumble,
   the lineage of love-kings labors in pain,
   making dust move again.

THE VISIT

I was fashioned in clay from clay,
in my blood embedded in the mold of living dust:
   bubblings of clinging clay,
   fermentation of slow creation,
   blaze of fired clay in the glimmer
   of transmutation,
   dissemination of powdered dust
   in the liberty of the dream,
   unstringing of chaos beads
   into pebbles,
   and steel solidity in the pupils
   of stones and sapphires.

I was wrenched up by the frenzy of fever;
the wild fierce birds lift me up
      and dash off . . .

in their craws I spy the affliction
of the realm and the vast earth . . .
a beat rises up and a flutter descends;
your door is the heavenly sphere, O my father,
and your clay gateway and the bolt
     are net and snare;
the slumber of birds when darkness
         lowers onto graveslabs,
         over the prickly pears of your grave,
         their chirpings in the arena of air,
         in blood's disclosure and sleep's revelation,
         are hidden calls from your dust
         and return calls from my dust,
         impossible to bring forth.

Bright is dawn
      suspended in the chandeliers of the *qasida*
as I kindle in the blaze of verdure
the sun rusted on the locks
of your door, O father.

I gave voice to the visit rite:
         how are the dust times?
         And how is the lineage
         fashioned from my dust?

I called out as the sparkling dawn
beneath the raven's wings
was inducing the wild birds
from nests moist with recollection,
for the celestial tours in the revelation
     of earth and blood,
from the start of your clay door
     until the end of my voice
     resounding with the call . . .

EARTH-REJOICING LAD

In your face the glow of blood
in which prophets are revealed and stallions neigh;
beneath the splitting legacy and demanding forefathers
is a spark in which windsteps are transformed:
speech rises up, strips off its meters, recalling the rites,
    rhymed prose sprouts in the murmurings of shamans
    and the blowing in knots of bast and reeds
    while the earth is brought forward
    and the sky is decreed water
    and the prophets—
                    completely rapt . . .

In your face a thousand bloods,
their decanters transparent;
while I am parceled from you into countries
I break myself loose
    into the dance and the dancers,
I flow and swell into torrents
    of progeny multiplying . . .
here is my body, one and many,
and here is the plight of the solitary:
a land jostling with creatures,
a pledge I confirm,
a journey of recollection,
a house for living,
rattlings of storms,
chewing of tender roots
    into the earth,
conversing with bird and beast,
the snarls of branches and tangles of water
    beneath my tongue . . .

I awaited . . .
    the voice roughens,
    the outgrown peach fuzz falls out,
    rapturing love grants tokens of its glory:

grass sheltering beneath the two arms,
a scent from which hidden calls
                    break into the open . . .
I hear the hoarse virility
and raptures in the footfalls of your sandals,
I hear in my body the shudder of the realm,
hear the footsteps of millions between my steps
                    and your steps . . .

I consecrated you: an offering
for buds flaring up in the wood of time,
and the sun dissolves
beneath the greenness of your shirt,
the dew hidden and the fire
        fill the earth with bygone ancestors,
fill my tanned face with the tribal *rajaz*
        of the desert,
and follow the steps of water
between *arac* and tamarisk;
        Canopus is your guide,
        and revelation, your hour . . .

The wedding—completed.
        Look! my blood turns to fine dust
        in the spheres of your love:
                I flow in the waters
                of the decanters between you two,
        I fold myself in the aroma of the cake . . .
Look! my blood in the banner
        of birds lodging in the horizon
        of the realms and the sea:
I lodge between the breastbones and the loins,
I become the inheritance and the inheritor . . .

Fire Joy

I.

Eons slipped by,
no way to discern beginnings from ends
apart from royal blood passed down
and his inner nature waging war against death
        by legacy,
overcoming the fall from throne
        by progeny,
and disseminating his traits
        in the lineage,
or by passing on canons and scepters
        to the inheritors.

One by one, seated on the throne,
        alive,
the last of them like the first,
fall away like the rest
                at the hour of death.
The king of the age kneels alone
flicking his eyes about the realm
of darkness, listening to shrieking
        splits
                of galaxies,
the expanding of earth
                as tombs detonate,
        histories roaring,
hearing clashes in his blood
and breath of eternities
                of desolate anticipation
        and caution,
observing how realms expanded, devouring
what belonged to him and to the heritage

of his lineage,
until it dwells in his blood
and skin,
he sees how expansion
—his own—
could send the outsiders ebbing
to far reaches,
imagined only.

When dawn approaches, he casts off his cloak,
takes up his war and hunting gear,
unbridles his mare
attentive to earthquaking jibes
harrassing his progress . . .
his limbs wheel round, his gear drips
from rust and fever-shake,
dawn's thrust seizes him with agonizing joy,
cool dew and the expanding earth
tempt him with the silence and the birds.

His calls rise up:

O age of loyalty scattered like wind,
have your unknown furies assaulted my frontiers
such that my throne legs are sunk in the span
between breathing in, breathing out,
or have the intruders ebbed,
so my kingdom's imagined reaches
become its beginning?

And loyalties . . . in their disputes,
have they opened slits in the horizon
so the sky is pouring banners and flags
on which blood totems rage?

And the lineage Hawk,
is there space for its flapping,
apart from sighs exhaled by the soul,
apart from punctures lanced in the neck?

Is it a quarry I chase in the hunt
or death weaving its murderous snares,
O age
                of
                        lo
                                lo
                                        yal
                                                yal
                                                        ties!
                                                                ties!
The king of the age comes
like all the kings of the lineage,
his gear, stab by stab, flashing their allure
while wound-springs ooze out
beneath his breastplate;
        he is broken up, his body pouring out;
        under his mare's hooves the sandy blood on earth:
                crescent tattoos . . .

Time for ceremonial burial:
        I, the inheritor of the age,
        wrapped him in his wounds,
        his gear enshrouding him,
        the dust of the bloodline,
        the sand, the silt, are sweet-smelling balms,
        laid him next to my grandfathers;
        the family reassembles in rows of martyrs,
        their tombs joined, one next to the other.

And I began my age:
        possessing throne and scepter;
        alone in my realm,
        no subjects but my ghost
        escaping in shade and light,
        mine the kingdom of contraries,
        a vision of seething possibilities
        grazed by madness in the garrison's wait
        in the maelstrom of tides . . .

I have . . . a woman:
sun crowns her head, cities of colors
open between her henna halos.
Around her navel scatter lofty stars.
She tossed aside two robes
of silt's ornaments—

one the robe of distances in light:

the soil wears it in a bud
breathing in the stone of possibilities,
swelling desires,
and heavy wombs wear it.

I grabbed her gift—
gifts being for such—
her face surrounded me,
            I am the river, she the banks.
Her dance scattered me,
            I am the lightning, she the wind.

The Hawk's shadow in the cloud
flutters between my eyelids,
its crimson flash splinters,
I read in its limbs the names
of my ancestors and my address—

 Mīm: A hand fettered in flaming silt;
            the forearm in naked basalt . . .
            pole of spark-flint in the dark,
            ruined country cavern.

 Ta': A phoenix waiting,
            sustained in the time
            of hay and firewood
            by readings of what the fire mare
            inscribed in the parchment
            of commandments.

Ra': The hoof's tattoo,
    fashioned by the vigil
    of demanding posts
    in the night of frontier ports.
    The bow drawn taut,
    the silver crescent,
    the spur between the horizon
    and the spring,
    ember tears between my eyelids.

The other, the robe of distance in night:

you are the domed space,
the tillage for me,
between us the water of the loins
and breastbones
bubbles with names.
I on your breast am two circles of red,
kohl-rimmed,
from my body to you I bequeathed a realm,
in turn you revealed yourself:

this is the horizon—
the sun smolders in its vents,
and sleep . . . a sycamore tree,
the birds taken by trees,
beneath the steps—
a cloud,
a lightning spark flying about
in the pollen shower,
as the river hides in the raisin
of your breasts.

I recall the soil of dikes
scripted by *mawwals* on the river's palm,
I recall . . .

MAWWAL FROM THE GARDENS OF A WOMAN

Ya layl, ya 'ayn, ya layl, ya 'ayn,
>   I am the steps,
>   in my blood is the path,
>   I'm the one sown by inscriptions
>   in the wind or dropped on peels,
>   snuffed out, falling in himself,
>   forehead banging on the rock,
>   making the unknown open the wall
>   between his face and the grave
>   in the kingdom of things.

Ya layl, ya 'ayn, ya layl, ya 'ayn,
>   I'm the one carrying
>   from the cities of horror
>   the treasure keys—
>   so you rise up: a swelled abyss
>   standing in my path,
>   and, in turn, I begin
>   the first of my embodiments
>   by falling into symbols.

Ya layl, ya 'ayn, ya layl, ya 'ayn,
>   in me linger scents
>   of watermoss and sparks
>   and the passion
>   for weaving on looms of names;
>   I carry on my fingers rings
>   of your soil simmering
>   with pristine mystery.
>   If I say *O trees!*
>   green buds burst out in the body
>   and fruits drop in my mouth.
>   If I say *O sky!*
>   in the spheres of eyes
>   stars of darkness and day
>   are rounded.
>   If I say *O creation!*
>   breast flowers and sunny fuzz
>   embody the quiver of cities

born from the union
of bloodlines and inscriptions.
Ya layl, ya 'ayn, ya layl, ya 'ayn,
delirium overwhelms me,
seasons of harvest lay heavy
on my memory,
my head, thick with power and poetry,
fell forward, I dozed . . .
my body: the opened-out earth;
creation: a fist of my clay;
the folk: my children;
Ya layl!

MAWWAL OF THE DISTANT GAZE

O ye who listen to my voice,
whenever black crows caw
in the hour of high forenoon,
whenever pitch darkness flutters
or an owl croaks in the decrepit perch,
responding to the modulations of my states
in the soul's wreckage—
O ye who listen to me,
my voice is a gazelle tattoo;
snakes wind in its charts,
ropes across ropes,
a weave laboriously
spidered together by storms.

The quarry is the last thing
my ruined dwellings preserved for me:
hearth's embers buried in its sand;
love, a mirage howdah on its desolation,
racing and beaming wherever I dwell or move,
Ya layl!

I make the call
only if I am listened to,
        or if I reach somebody . . .

The rolling out of the river
on the soil of speech:
        nothing but a land of clay's blood;
the earth dozed under the glass of darkness,
        melting in it,
when the young mare of the *arghoul* unloosed
the taut bridle;
        the bard,
at the breakup of the guests and the wedding party,
        wept his love, year after year.
        Ya layl, ya 'ayn, ya layl, ya 'ayn, ah,
the mysterious face of country
fashioned by the vision:
        tangles of birds in storming clouds,
and the river rising, its banks
        a mercy of deep sleep.
The waterwheels sleep only
in the wound and blood
lodged in the clay
and weaning-bread *mawwal,*
        Ya layl, ya 'ayn, ya layl, ya 'ayn, ah,
I am listened to,
only if I reach somebody . . .
ghosts on the river bluffs
and dove nests decorated with blood
between the steps and the silt,
a dawn of blood floated on the river
eddying out its arms and garments
and a face from death-swaddles peeked out,
        Ya layl, ya 'ayn, ya layl, ya 'ayn, ah,
        the bard floating on the water,
        the heavy-stepping river dragging him
        from folk to folk, year to year.
I will reach somebody . . . only if

the mysteriously fashioned face
of the country
suddenly appears from the clay of words!
Yā layl, ya ʿayn, ya layl, ya ʿayn, ah.

II.

For whom is this earth,
this usurped land, its grape clusters
one by one made to fall,
this land stormed by countries league on league,
its open spaces hedgehogged by spears,
this land unstrung from wounds
like some prey run down in the palms

. . . for whom?

I wore my dread as a gown.
I said to myself: the fort of writing
where stallions of transmuted blood gather
is the solitary king's last resort . . .

The age:
a pack of dogs in heat,
frenzied by scribblings,
snapping, growling, making to mount,
while the royal cadaver was falling apart,
earth celebrating instinct's night
with grilled human blood.

Such barking has its price:

i.

The right sense of words falls out,
the hot lust of scribbling collapses.
Distances stay deserted
and the fearsome stallions arrive.
Ghastly countenances arrive.

ii.

The flesh of dictionaries
drips off their frail spines.
The verb's corpse is divulged
in the wood formula of coffins,
and the noun harbors the void's
      bitter cold;
significance irrevocably divorced
from allusion and sense,
grammar trades around its terms;
speech remains a distance of sand
throughout which dummies and invading armies
      stand posted.

iii.

If in the inscriptions
horizon's vent extended
between *taqiyya* and the secret,
between the mask and symbols' endurance,
then do grow large, O sun,
in the gloom of nightmares.

Do weave, O quiver, the blood knot
for labor's sudden pains—
O quiver of the promising womb.

iv.

The land of despots was a carpet,
fissures cracking up its arboreal patterns,
rolled up tight before the invaders . . .
rolled up . . . then its towers started to rise,
a land of sand and wind stretched out.

The bard chanted:
      Grant the face of the stone
      the sanctity of your steps
      then go forth and pen a homeland
      ripping open like a wound.

There was chatter
as the Mamlukes divided up the loaf
        of slavery,
brute words resounding like death traces
written on my forehead,
flipped by lightning and thunder
until the labor pains of sudden fire.

                v.

Water flaming now in the river . . .
how might deliverance come,
with or against the current, O swimmers,
while ships wreck, disintegrate,
and no defender?
Stepping is drowning,
and the distance between me and my realm,
my throne, is blood and fire crocodiles!

                vi.

I behold . . .
the sunstep broader than calamity's realm,
deeper than peels of rust
condensed on the loaf of earth,
farther than reaches imagined,
closer than breath in a pair of lungs.

I behold the sunstep . . .
the earth—its spur;
the swift wind—its mare.
O sun of nightmares, strike
in the wood of the throne,
        let the worms in,
for earth is a gate
and death leads the way
        in the land.
The sudden fire: a whirlwind
in the horizon of possibilities,
and the sun hurries . . .

continents fleeing beneath it.
The sand script twines with water letters,
the flying leaves gather in the Book of creation,
the sun hurries more distantly from us
and more closely.
The age raises its chaotic fires
bearing the signs of its exile:
homelands for births and possibilities . . .
the sun hurries more distantly
from us and more closely.

III.

Are you fleeing naked under the peels of space
or are you emerging covered up
       like a breast?
Are you a crown of hay worn by the king
       of the age
awaiting the strike of lightning,
the flash of sudden fire?
Or are you a rhyme smoldering under ashes
       of speech?
And are these distances your ripping *sirwal*
       beneath which creatures fester,
       flesh dressing their entombed bones?
Or are you a swallow,
       an ember moving from bough to bough
             of the senses,
       opening up in the wood of legacy
       a doorway for clouds
       and bringing spring stallions
       to neigh in the body of the earth?
Are you one,
and the cosmos but the names
       of your face?

Or are you a sycamore in cosmic space,
your green leaves exuding the taste of land,
your shade housing the sacred marriage
while water and silt in your living root crowd?

Rise in the radiance of resurrection,
rise up from my blood . . .
      O you, the sob of sudden possibility!
      O joy of questioning!

These are the swallows of your embers written down . . .
    all is but a cage and a horizon opened up by the dream—
sleeping and roped down are you, with knotted braids;
between your breasts slumber is pouring out,
water and silt are your spreads,
the wind inscribed in the cries of *mawwals* . . .
rise, rise up from my blood . . .
you sleep on,
round your waist runs a string
of villages and cities
. . . you are stretched out
    —all is but a bed and a storm rubbing the eyes after a doze—
and your face, arcades in the ruins of kingdoms . . .
this is me, king of the age . . .
on my mats creation gathers,
I enter every home,
my subjects in each one.
I wear the silt of villages as a ring, and a tongue
for the might of my heart as a passage
to my country, which will witness
      this scepter someday spinning wind, land, and sea . . .
      eat then from what you have sown,
      celebrate the feasts of my testament . . .
      for here fire scatters its robes
      extending its steps through the joy of questions
      yielding their forms in the mirrors
            of the country . . .

Water Boy

THE PREDICATE IN ADVANCE

I wrap myself with sunshine,
    with dusty horizons,
I cleanse my body with hay,
    with pointed blades of grass,
I lather it with anger.
    I unseal the wind,
    reveal hidden dew in buds.
Bees dwell under my arms,
    frightened springs hide
    between my fingers.
The earth is a glass
    smashing spectral colors,
    strewing them
on my body suspended
    between hunger and spring.
I grow full bit by bit,
    like the dangling, reddish winter squash
    on sand pyramids, on scorched mastabas.
I ripen slowly,
S
  L
    O
      W
        L
          Y
I rejoice in my coming of age,
    in the revelations of my blood.
To children I am a rolling, radiant globe,
to despots, an encroaching, mined conspiracy,
to misty seekers, a riddle forever haunting.

While you, woman, under my eyes—
      a tillage, curving and furrowing—
whenever we will together,
    we become Will;
between our two navels
      breadloaves await the inheritors.

Here is water, water, water!
Water is a portal whose locks
     night opens
for the passage of creation:
      seas embracing seas,
      springs marrying springs;
      the river pulls out the wedding kerchief
      embroidered with dinars and foliage,
      dispersing earrings and bracelets.

Water is a portal whose locks
     dawn also opens:
     here is God saluting,
     dispatching trees and letters
     in lines and lines of scriptural space.

I cast off the robes of my blood . . .
the net of its names shaping
     the capturing moment.
He stayed me, in the wonder
     of sprouting wheat,
so as to warm to birds,
     and they to me.
O birds, descend with the peace
     of gliding clouds!
     Do descend!
I tie together the heart-felt joys,
     sprout by sprout . . .

such is the capturing moment:
flocks of doves enter my memory's towers;
each dove weaves a word nest

by the grace of its script;
     it is the birds . . .

The sea amasses sleep under sheets,
     under dark verdure,
playing with the sun of nightmares
     and time, in memory's bed.
The sea's wrist . . . braceleted by earth.
Vast continents are drawn onto its waves:
     here is the earth,
     an urn of crumbly ashes
     decorated with scarabs and horses.
The names of those who possessed its scepters
are inscribed on crumbled thronic coffins.
On its broken potteries distant kisses
     still flame,
and steps on the granite surface cry out
between ruined columns and the hall;
gods speak in prayer books: *Listen!*

Here is the sea, slipping on the earth's bracelet,
slipping it off;
sea nymphs open up for me roads
to the sublime moment: darkly green
or branched with grey silk and crimson.
The midday sky is pierced,
cosmic gold plunges into the water,
the sea opens the locks of its coffers:
     gold descending . . .
     gold ascending . . .
domes on the edge of the water
cast off the robes of their fugitive desires,
     eject their cries.

Are you departing when brute gold
at the moment of tide erects cities and towers,
clutters the water with metal herds,
as doves plummet from such deathly horizons?

Or are you washing the robes of your voice
in water books, waiting for the sea,
       walking on its face, matching
          —at the cry of time and of cities awakening for death—
          the turf under your feet and the way,
          as it stretches its carpets,
          rocking the realm of sleep
          and the fresh, uncontained language
          lying at the bottom?

I cast off the robes of my blood . . .
thick with the nouns of exile
          growing like palm trees,
seeping through clasped hands,
between lowered eyelids, in whispers.
The verbs of death are masked
          with crumbly ashes . . .

       I depart . . .
this is the dance . . . I see it:
a body whose rhythm branches into agility
          and violence;
here is my body breaking up
          with hovering wonder
as water turns me into water,
and I robe it with my cry,
my body the sea-body; between us
a living rose blooms,
enticing my blood with the fusion
          of death and virility.

I depart . . . the sea is my capital,
          my road,
I share its deep cravings for migration
          through the body of the earth.
Will the cities awakening for death
          open their portals
for the mail of wounding letters
          traveling between me and the tribe?

I slowly assault their walls
        between noon's repose
and the circling hyenas of dream.

Water . . .
and this is the throne,
man's chair stretching between two waters,
flanking the vast homeland
canopied by night's loose turban
        and day's columns,
            full with modulations of chiaroscuro.
This is man's chair;
in its filigree nests a verdant dove
        with white-ringed ankles,
in motherly glow until the promised day.
        I talk to her, she talks to me.
She circles over the water's face.

        Behold!
Foam and open shells reveal a woman.
A shooting star lit her seven kingdoms.
Camel-clouds, knitted with glowing veins,
        trembled overhead,
                passing in caravans,
and on earth stumps of palm trees
took the shape of men
        lined up in her kingdoms.
The clouds flash their lanterns
through slits in celestial darkness.
        Sand, by the flare of dream,
            reveals a woman, braids glittering
            with lightning-fish and water;
the horizon ruptures beneath her steps . . .
she descends.
On earth, stumps of palm trees
        take the shape of men;
the woman of water and lightning descends . . .
        O woman, from what clay,
            fired by fate into potterware,

from what vessel
did your wet fire
leak out and filter
    limb by limb,
flipping between my hands
    your seven gardens,
and in my bed,
your flaming buds blossom,
    making us blood-ready
    for harvest?

AMBIGUOUS TERMS

The tribe possesses ashen fires . . .
from fire substance there is nothing but blood embers
    in the ash of memory;
the hospitality rite: aromas of *tharida*,
    coffee, and cardamom
clank in the *qasida*'s remains;
dream horrors snatch women's sleep:
glassy sky, black crows gyrating a storm
  . . . banging the sky, piercing it,
bloody tatters falling out on the birds
and horses, their necks flinging about,
the bleeding spurting higher, higher . . .

At the cry of vision women raised their eyelids:
    the earth is a space cracking
    from the thirst of a too long season,
    while low suns lash at parched fronds.
    Grass is but sand scattered by scorching wind
        in the camp . . .
    the camel-hair tent exposed, thin and torn.
    In the redness of eyes and whiteness of salted lips
    the sun of famine has melted.

The folk retreated from the infernal sun to hell's sand,
passing round chatter-loaves and devouring talk,
remembrance dialects gnawing their livers,
their hands searching out ember-pebbles
to sketch out on sand their fortunes and waymarks,
inciting the women soothsayers
to the old ways of tracking and bird portents.
      Flaming hunks of sun grow closer . . .

The folk burdened me with suns
capable of melting lizards and jerboas,
my she-camel: thirst stacked high by histories.
My body: the only food I had.
And I, in the tribe's tradition,
keep company with the ghoul,
listen to the roars of she-demons
      lusting for he-jinns . . .
for I bear the rhymed oath, the hard covenant,
while the river has the face of the quarry
      amid the desert's mirages.

My elect state overwhelmed me:
      I was seized by the yield
      of the senses,
      and the signs of epiphany,

. . . the earth book tumbled through myriad exegeses.

Then from the rust of letters
I gathered up the sense and a field of vision . . .

      The homeland has wet edges covered by water:
            undone braids in the sea
            crusted with silver salt crystals,
            the head is all aflame with hoariness
            and menses not yet ceased.
      Among the toes of its relaxed feet crayfish,

jellyfish, and shellfish breed,
and the glue of copulating reptiles
and glowing grass . . .
still, a certain distance of blood
between foot and step
that's not forthcoming.
An infected mouth:
on its lips the pus of words form
and birds nest in its cracked teeth
. . . moss and palm trees sprout
on the leftovers of the prey.
Between it and the voicing
resides a distance
of an extinguished cry
in memory, not surging.
Knotted fingers of two hands drop
henna and grease,
inflaming the instincts of sharks,
drawing whales 'round the torn meat
reddened with sappanwood and jujube.

Here is the shape of such a country:
a shrouded body borne up
by lumps of petrol ooze,
by fermented lineage bones,
by the dung of the worldly spoiled.
The sun gouges out its eyes.
Is there no water?
Nay, is there no joy in its
fantasy?
Nay, no fantasy
of finding it in a bog
here or there?

Yea, there is water and a soaking body
—yet neither drowning nor drinking.
Perished indeed alike, the seeker and the sought.

Soldiers swept me away . . .
woman, your father's palace is by the river:
in the marble columns
          colors vein together;
your steps resounded in the domes
          like dove chants
and the squeezed sky dripped amidst
          the chandeliers
. . . a river and a sun both prisoners
          in your ceiling!

I said to myself: I am finished
                    yet barely begun . . .
my good tidings of grass and water
have not reached the tribe.

        But as for him who was given his promise, choking inwardly;
            when he is cast into a narrow place, coupled in fetters,
                    his chains will rattle, and he shall roast
                            on carping regrets
                            on shrieking fires
                            on blazing sorrows.

The folk are deciphering the sand,
            drawing and erasing,
            and if they could find a shelter,
            a cave or an entry,
they would have turned to it,
            having lost hope and weakening.
Who will redeem me with a leafing cry,
            or a dream's herb that greens out
            in the graceful mercies of interpretations
            or in the cloud of auspicious rain!
Perished indeed alike, the seeker and the sought.

And I said to myself:
Bear the woe of Barmecide courtiers;
it will only be relieved in vales
            of Arabia . . .

suddenly out of such dust, banners will soar,
       of blood unavenged
whose thirst quenching has been delayed.
       The battle cry
       may emerge from their mouths . . .

I said to myself:
       Bear the woe of the Barmecides,
       heavy on your wrists and ankles
       though their fetters be,
       filled with grasping greed
       though they are . . .
       bear what you see of conspiring intents,
       of duping pomposity . . .

I said to myself:
       Bear their prosperous faces
          dripping health,
       bloody opulence, and possession
          of earth's back.
       Bear what you see:
          the indolent and the wanton,
          the dandy and the haughty.
       Their palace is a throning coffin;
       and it is your exile overflowing with dread,
       your imprisonment
       within petrifying thirst,
       within a flood of anxiety;
       it is the fetters
       biting wrists and ankles . . .

Humming iron and rattling metallic leaves
       of armor-clad troops . . .
the clouds that swept me up,
       dispersed in the monster scene:
your face breaking out from the crack of morn,
       drawing closer and closer like the gleam
       in a cloud in the desert of the tribe . . .
you, the water moon moored in Barmecide marble!
       And throngs were lined up in rows . . .

when we fused in blood
and you saved with a nod of your head
       the prisoner,
and promoted my rank and crowned me
with your appearance in the nude,
and wriggled between my daze
       and my fear,
I approached   I distanced myself:
       the difficult oath was shining
       in the night of its rhymes,
       extending between me and you
       the horizon of tents . . .
in that waste the camel-hair tent surged
and a cloud knotted of splintering locusts,
revealing the motifs of carpets,
the tremors of silk flood ebbing languidly,
presenting the ruins of a rain-racked sky . . .
       shining silver crescents
       from the trotting sound,
       hooves of the mares
       hooking them side by side . . .
       their echoes falling away,
       not yet extinguished,
       linking a continuous chain,
       connecting the last step
       with road's beginning,
       with sighs of rhymed farewells,
       with the humming of diviners,
       with the designs of sand-writing
       in the fire-scorched motifs,
       branching with thirst,
       with the flabbiness
              of death
       roofed over with ashes,
       with sun's splinters,

       with the lightnings of crows,
       wrecking down the cadaver.

How then, when voice and echo
are circles woven together
      rising and rising
      until throbbing with heartbeats
      and shivers of a body
      folded and unfolded
      by dread and desire . . . how then?

And how a   howdah   marble   moon?

SUBJECT DEFERRED

Shocked awake by the vision in himself,
and in the horizons,
he said to himself:
      Isn't the earth wide open, the land ripe
      for night journeying and midday halting?
He emerged from weeping and took on
the pilgrim's attire,
girded himself up with knowledge
      of his blood,
the surge for martyrdom and the power
      of inner nature
stripped of all reward,
      all ambition.

Such is birth. He knows its gingery taste,
its coffee-like smack in the nostrils,
he recognizes the nature of its flowing messages.
. . . Such are good tidings:
      throngs, eyes fixed,
      waves bestriding waves,
      intuition spreading like anxiety,
      clamor bellowing,
      banners flapping,
      the foam of color's mirth,

the mighty tiding escaping
from the frontiers
of speech and the net
of incisive composing.

His woman said:
    Of what do they question one another?
He answered:
       Those that were before them were contrived;
    then God came upon their building from the foundations,
      and the roof fell down on them from over them,
        and the chastisement came upon them
          from whence they were not aware.
She said:
    Sorrow not . . . isn't the earth wide open?
He said:
    Let that which made them haughty
    and all their earthly possessions
    fall down. Let the people's
    anger crush them for their crimes.
She said:
    Your ancestors' voice torments you,
    listen to them with obedient attention.
    They will restore you to a place of homing:
    tasting of coffee,
    redolent of cardamom
    and firewood of the tribe.
    Command the verbal knot now!
    Let metaphor fill you.

He said:
    If earth won't let me flow,
    rebel I will against it,
    raising with sly metaphors
    the means for my friends to recognize
    me, and I to recognize them.
    When the time arrives,
    the vales will fill with us.

She said:

> Here night comes to its middle;
> will you be the destroyer
> of what they commanded of tricks,
> no matter how well constructed,
> the darkness like a steel tower
> or the glow of brandished sword from afar
> with its clamor and echo?

> > Were it a gain near at hand, and an easy journey,
> > they would have followed thee.

1.

I said:

> O water moon . . . an infatuation knot
> is between you and me.

> A camel-cloud pulls its loop,
> drawing its hooves from my blood
> to the skies,
> > raising your position
> in the clan at earth's end.

> Ancient mothers possess bird-shaped and crescent tattoos,
> their earrings: rust dripping tears. Their gems
> are swung in braids aflame with hoariness
> by the long-gone glitter of pollen dust.

This is me and your dispersal in my hands:
kingdoms of desire and bewilderment,
your bed aflame with unsuspected thrones
while the night—embers of galaxies and dreams.

I said to myself:

> The reading of sand-marks,
> deciphering word pebbles,
> the winds chasing,
> not leaving me in concealment
> > with my glory
> of seductive and rapturous love.

Poetry surges in my bones: a gazelle of thorns
running in the desert with the swiftness
        of an echo,
my memory bleeds . . .

My love is ascending with the Yemen caravan,
my body is in Mecca in chains.
But once she came eddying toward me
the bars were fast but she came,
came and gave me greeting, and rose
and turned and pivoted my life that way.
My head is bent not for death or anything.
I am not tired of the gyves, my soul
is immune to the loud promises.
Only a longing for the days has disarmed me,
the days when we met and I was free.

        2.

I saw the sense in my dream,
        this madness of those-who-have-nothing
                dense with love passion,
        and royalty and bloody gold,
        tempting me with a body for metaphors,
        a soul for the flash of anklets,
        a bracelet for the fetters biting
        on my wrists, a poor madness indeed,
                I thought,
        falsifying the ciphering
        of pebbles and writing in the sand.

Let them behold:
        a slave queen caught by a princely slave,
        a whale of purple marble
        carrying on its golden veins and flippers
        a sea of abundance and a boat—
        a silver vessel lingering on the water;
        between sky and clouds, a bed.

I worried the folk might recognize me,
I falsified the signs written on sand,
I obscured what they read
and came in the finery of love passion
preparing my body like a corpse,
embalming and perfumes to delay
the disclosure of death,
extravagant gentleness and slow stepping,
and swaddles of multihued ornament,
splendor of silk shrouds.

And you tamed me with promises of resurrection
of our bodies and the body of time,
you flipped me between two states:
       of love passion in the marble of kingdom,
       and of glory in the kingdom
       of those-who-have-nothing madness . . .

       3.
—Is this the return to the beginning?

       — Yes, it is the return to the beginning.

—How? since you have turned into a name
       among others
and your trees have wood in the hearths
and aroma in the feast set for crowded guests!

       — In the beginning I was
       between my mother and my father,
       a name among many names
       of the dream,
       a rite among many rites
       of water
       performed in the twilight
       before sunrise
       with earthen pitchers
       with incense

with traces of henna on the heels.
The short *suras* were joined like a tent
in the harmonies of youth,
in the rhythms of the white forenoon
and the brooding night.

It is the return to the beginning;
night and day are gates on the kingdom's road,
my father on my right,
on my left my mother,
while the country discards
its immature accents,
reaching the platform
to voice promises and threats,
extending itself into a mat
against fear and hunger,
into a pillow against nightmares.

Water is the ember of recollection;
I blow on it, look into
what is beyond the ornament of rock,
the marble of metaphor,
so as to witness how the glory
of gushing springs is.

In your braids a knot
came loose in my palms:
sparrows of henna and perfume
entranced me with a specter of vertigo,
and a tremor, no sooner than it seized me up
I spied *Canopus* glancing at me
from her braided locks,
as dozing sleep swayed
the chandelier hanging over the bed.

A cloud passed by
opening its buttonholes,
undoing the buttons,
hiding itself in the glass of skies,

and flash by flash was revealed
weaving a crown of new fronds;
between its two hands blows
sparkling sand,
and birds storm.
Between skies water pours
in a domed shape spreading in the distance
two wings of the darkness of flood.
Is it a camel-cloud thundering her cry,
waking us by marble of the palace
lifting its feet out of their footholds,
raising its anchor,
gathering its petrified steps
from the stone quarry of the earth,
raising columns of smoke and dust
undulating in the wind?
Is it a camel-cloud braying with thunder
and the ruined arcades trembling
            with water,
shaking the royal howdah,
causing chains to fall,
the earth becoming an abyss?

Or did I sort out my vision
so your bed blazed
with nightmarish madness of metaphors!

Air Joy

Now is that singular time for the onset
of beginning or the last of ending—

everything ends:
        they are two bodies on a spot of blood,
        a magic killing; she is killed
            and he is killed.
Who between the two aimed the blade?
Who between the two initiated the act
        and the passion?

It is the one stab.

Who between the two was ablaze
        in the burning ember,
        by a kiss sneaking up
        until the mixing
        of the vigorous blood;
        or by a cry of ecstasy
        meshing its *ah* with death?

In whom between the two springs
cracking open:
        this father constantly succeeding
            amidst the ribs?
        Or the mercy hidden
            in the promising womb!

And the postponed one . . .
        even if the life span is snapping,
        even if the fantasy recedes . . .
the body of the weary woman neither answers

the fiery blood with fire of her own
nor takes pity on the sparkling thirst
in the goblet with water,
in the clay with dream,
in the sleep with flight to the sun,
and the hesitating mouthful
in the wheat with poetry,
and the homeland whose taste
dissolves in the spittle of seizure
with magic,
and the stiff corpse with the last bond
of lightning-dance,
which the wind surprised the soul with.

This is the one stab—
the moment of decision let go of it,
time flaunting passion, playing with it
fast and loose.

She covered herself—while viewers
were passing on in buses and spilling
onto the cobblestone of pursuits,
no man-viewer gazing

amidst the kohl, and shining ripples
under the two sashes and the Bedouin dance

at the flash of blade, no woman-viewer
stripping bare the steps from the course
—climbing to death with passion—
not detecting the flame of madness
of metaphors in the clay of the face,
as she is confounded
between an eloquent silence
and a chatter with splintered allusions.

The early winter morning was throwing about
its handkerchiefs of light drizzle;
flutter of clouds amid drowsy branches;
vestiges of sleep were under the kohl powder,

and the flagging vigil erupting in flashes,
making the steps rattle; and he—entranced,
        wakeful.

The morning was moist with dew and mist,
opening in the desolation of earth and soul
                a rent . . .
distant sky translucid, and the roaming birds
were perfecting the forms of their joy
                and calls . . .

That was the forenoon prayer:
        flows of creation stood in rows,
        invigorated by collective ablution;
creation was under the profound space
                rising,
their steps and frames running parallel
                between two lines . . .
a house for all, the earth,
a dream for all, the horizon,
justice for all, the joy whose colors are aroused
in the fountains of birds, weaving and reweaving
                heavens and serenity . . .
laudation of *Allahu Akbar*
from the resounding revelations
and the inspiration raised by the verdure
        of the living;
the turning of craned anxiety under the surfaces
        of matter;
the rhythm of the pains
of possible sculptures in the rock,
of the mouth watering with poetic stirrings
in the knot of the bosom amid the petals,
of the raptures caused by ripening pleasure
in the dropping fruit onto the down of grass.
The ardor of creation is moistened
in the crowd's prostration by the tears
        of intimation;
the supplications rise with the breath
        of morn and earth;

my blood rises in the resounding litany,
      water with water,
      clay with clay formed;
the rock moans with it;
      ornaments branching in the mirth of birds
      silently becoming poetry and the fugitive sigh;
and your eyes from the insomnia of kohl
      and nacreous quicksilver
      are eloquent silence,
      and a chatter whose allusions splinter;
      and I, the pure gasp . . .

—From whom? From where?

      —No land. No time.
      I have left them behind.
      I am nothing but a moan from prime matter;
      but a drop of blood stranded
      beneath the hand of God
      as He flips it at His will
      on a thirst blazing, or knotting grief.

—How then did the silt of your face
      quench its thirst by me:
      it is the silt of my country!
      And what hand dug onto your forehead
      my inscribed song of youthful days
      or dispersed in the glitter of your wild gray hair
      what the horizon could not contain
      of defiance-stallions,
      and what the bygone visions
      sensed blurringly of passion
         and denudation
      beneath the hand of God?

      —From what persistent embers and fragile age
      do you set this morning on the throne,
      the *fatiha* in the prayer of creation,
      while God blows from the spirit
      of His names alerting wonders!

The sky of the city is washed,
dangling the chandelier of day
and the lamp of awakening at night,
extending its streets from its broken tiles
and cobbles, a step tempting with it pursuit,
or a step infatuating the insight . . .
rising lightly, lightly—then trembling,
amid the visions and dispersed blood,
        a land tempted by us.
It steps along our steps and opens the hall
        of kingdoms:
a carpet flipping in its body
        the tremor of spirit,
a fountain of birds and fresh leaves,
the glare of midday and hunt,
a wound and sand-wind in the wastelands,
the tumult of she-gazelles, stallions
and arcades for kings
and silence surrounding the curtains
        of the harem pavilion,
and silence surrounding the passage
leading to the throne hall;

we had reached the hall . . .
I am not of me and you are not of you,
while Al-Wasiti had freed the camels
        of his paintings
to drink water from your palms
and commence their reverberations
with earth-moving yearning.

                —Will this cold sip turn the herd of camels
                    to Al-Wasiti, turbaned by the sun,
                    into a dream and a bond
                    between his brush and heavens!
                    Will the sip recover the herd
                    of the *mawwals* in the thirst
                    of forty!

—Listen . . .

you are a guest at the mercy of clouds . . .
invoke the wind and be silent . . .
for the mercy of the clouds will descend
on no one save he who perfects silence
    and waiting . . .
listen . . .
the wind is chanting the litanies
of its *hals*,
hummings of births in the legacy,
the rite of quenching creation's thirst
between heaven and earth
with the immortal awe,
in front of space extending
and the ember in the heart
of those who perfect their waitings,
and they will be granted the gift
of hearing how creation undergoes
the pains of its joys and births.
It is passion in the Book
of the cosmos
and it is the *qasida* in the mud
of creation . . .
so listen.

From silence elapsed a long night;
upon me descended from the gifts
of hospitality my good tidings.
My lady, is it my blood in the decanters
or your shawl ornamented with heavens
and earth spreading over the table?
Then your subjects arrive,
two of every kind, the earth is brought
forward in the ceremony of love
    and revelation!

Tears have dissolved me into a silt
    from the silt.

—Are you the country fermented in the visions,
   which none save it gave me birth?

                    —And you are the country that knotted me
                       into a lump of flesh in its womb,
                       then animated the creation out of me,
                       and it blasted marveling at its youth.

—Blood into blood
   or water-quakes crushing in the layers
   of recollection and dream!
   Camels reverberating from the cracking thirst
   or a cry fidgeting in the delapidation
   of age amid the ruins!

                    —I am the acacia pole . . .
                       the tents of the clan were wearing out,
                       swept by storms one by one,
                       and I remain . . .
                       gathering in my frame,
                       reverberated by the wind,
                       the recollections of sheltered spouses
                       and stallions.

—My shawl is a cover and a camel-hair tent
   fluttering in your hand.

                    —And you are a land with low plains
                       for water and grass.

—You are the heaven of serenity,
   you are the fugitive bard
   among the herds of my love . . .

A night of figurative talks and silence passed;
the dawn was spreading its twilight,
folding forty mats—the age—

of ruins and remains of ashes in the hearths,
until I was revealed alone; and I gazed out . . .
the steppes of the clan were desolate . . .
and I, the acacia pole beneath its skies,
detected a passion howdah appearing,
a camel-hair tent, and a desert breaking out
        with grass ember buds . . .

I said:
        Listen . . .
the herds of your love rise in the dew
of the dawn, bleating,
and the singer gathers the rhythm
        of his *mawwal*
from the steps of the wind . . .

She said:
For him a night to forget what he has seen . . .
        so listen . . .

A sun penetrates the palm fronds
stroking the curtains behind the glass . . .
our appointment is the silence of night
granted by the spirit-flash
between heavens and earth
        and the choking gasp . . .

The bard sings . . .
and the sigh of his *mawwal* split into weeping lament
and a flashing of the east wind
pulling with its train the lavender of the clan,
girding itself with braids of pomegranate blossom
with blooming basil in the parting of the hair,
refreshing itself in flaming meadows
robust with hearty verdure.

He sings . . .
or is it the dream?
Or the land of glory from blood and poverty?

Or an amorous fling from heaven descending!
Dawn sparkling in the longing of the heart?
Or passion beneath whose muddle
histories are illuminated?
Or blood looking longingly to the glow
of its minarets?

                                    Exile . . .

or is it petrified thirst
cracking into sand deserts,
distancing their distances?
Or playground for jinn and beast
whose courses the wind inscribes?
            Or is the bard singing?

I am the acacia pole . . .
in my bearing, the pride of expectation;
in my body, the pride of kings
to whom are granted in the course of the lineage
signs of their race between the silence
of ashes and auspicious winds.

In the glory of my selection by you,
the clan-deserts were rising toward the luminosity
            of the dream;
your herds were dispersing,
and the *mawwals* were in the unrestrained wind
and in the silence unloosed.
I said:
            From where?
            Whither the steps go?
            Which generating foot will crack my voice,
                        opening up
            in the flood of visions
            and the density of its beat
            the guise of returning rain
            splitting with verdure!

That night you were a mask
whose evocations revealed talismans

of an ancient glory of love
assigned to oblivion,
and a country and columns of marble
and sand and prayers.
You figured in my desire
and rose out of bottles of perfume
aged in the eternity of the Orient:
rosebuds of silk transparent,
flashing loot from the vigil
of the Select.
A hand is my tremor,
and my desire is a hand,
and the metaphor of the clan
is shedding its diaphanous gowns.
From the plundered treasures I have
a flashing gem;
I untie the silks of your virginal charms;
I wrap myself in their magic
and pick up from them the gifts
of her marvels, fold by fold . . .
and the signs are unveiling their figures;
I was seized by lightnings of passion
and dread,
and a sigh was sparked coming down
with the thundering wonder;
and your palms of merciful clouds
were exchanging blood for blood,
one heaven for another,
inscribing on my forehead a land,
erasing age,
and pollen was in the palm tree of beginnings;
and the dawn . . .
tenderness was dew dripping into my clay;
the warmth of your hands was gathering
what was scattered of piled-up birth scars
and moles, marks of craving-denied old mothers,
sprinkling what gets unstrung
from the beads of the back,
kindling in the bone and flesh
the fantasies of free flight . . .

I become light; you become light;
neither are you from you,
        nor I from me;
we have ripened into one blood . . .

—One dead,
    how will death be split
    into two corpses?

                    —It is one corpse.

—What if the kin fought to fill
    two dust holes with one dust
    gathered by love in the prostration
    of passion?

                —Soft is the clay step in the clay:
                    beneath us the earth gathers into a carpet,
                    dust flinging upon dust;
                    and in the passion prostration
                    the blood of the man prostrating
                    does not reveal the blood of the woman prostrator;
                    one blood runs aground in the darkness
                    of the earth
                    beneath the hand of God,
                    then tossed by the wind
                    in the hand of omnipotence;
                    it rises lightly, taking its course
                    in the radiant mystery
                    of its nocturnal journeys,
                    largely, as the frame
                    of the universe exacts,
                    narrower than the sigh of spirit
                    in spirit.

Between heavens and earth
the wind was tempted by us,
for it steps along our steps,
and we step along its steps;
space is the dance of our temptations . . .

and the minarets are poles of our tent;
the domes are our hands relaxing;
the deserts are nap pillows,
and the temples bear the form
of our fingers in their tangles
        at the moment of dream . . .
we are the shirt spangled
with flowering stars and fresh trees
        and houses;
we are the destined void between the galaxies
and the ecstatic melody
        in the course of planets;
we are the blasting forth of civilizations
        in the primal language;
our commencement is the pure sigh;
our end, the pure generating beat . . .

Glossary

alif:	The name of the first letter of the Arabic alphabet.
Allahu Akbar:	An Arabic locution that means "God is the Greatest." It is used in prayers and in the call for prayers.
arac:	A tree whose bark *(siwak)* is used for tooth brushing *(miswak)*.
arghoul:	A folk wind instrument used in Egypt, consisting of one pipe or two pipes of unequal length. It is related to the clarinet and used in popular festivities.
'ayn:	Eye; literally in the sense of the sight organ and metaphorically in the sense of the heart or center.
Barmecide: (Barmakid)	Refers to the Barmaki family of viziers who served the 'Abbasid caliphs and became very powerful. They flaunted their wealth and became arrogant. They have been associated historically (and imaginatively in the *Arabian Nights*) with the eighth-century caliph Harun al-Rashid and his reign in Baghdad.
Canopus:	A star in the constellation of Argo.
dinar:	Originally an Islamic gold coin used as a currency unit (although now the word is used to indicate paper currency in some Arab countries). The golden dinar is often used as decoration for veils or as a pendant.
fasila:	The special end rhymes of Koranic verses *(ayat)*.
fatiha:	It is, literally, a prelude or opening. Religiously, it is used to refer to the first chapter *(sura)* of the Koran.
ghoul:	A fabulous and dangerous creature in Arabian lore.
hal:	In (Jurjani's) Sufi lexicon, it is an "elect state" that befalls a mystic and is temporary. It is differentiated from "elect station" *(maqam)*, which is attained by application and effort. *Hal* is characterized by joy, sorrow, or exaltation.
henna:	A plant whose leaves and flowers are used as cosmetic dye and occasionally for medical and prophylactic purposes (against the evil eye). It is particularly associated with brides, who use it to decorate their hands and feet in a ceremony of ritual dyeing.
howdah:	The curtained seat or litter on the back of a camel, traditionally used for carrying women in nomadic moves. Presently, it is associated with transporting a bride.

jinn: Pre-Adamic beings created from smokeless fire, hence often invisible. Although some of them may be pious, they are mostly associated with rebellion and satanic evil.

kohl: An eye cosmetic often identified with antimony sulfide, but it may include other substances. It is usually ground and used as a fine powder to paint on the eyelids or around the eye.

layl: The word means night, and it is often modulated in interpretative free songs to indicate grief and affliction.

Mamluke: Literally means slave. It refers to rulers of slave origin who governed in Egypt and Syria from the end of the thirteenth century to the beginning of the sixteenth century. Their empire was associated with bloody struggles for succession. The military intrigues and pettiness of these slave-rulers were proverbial.

mastaba: A term used in Egyptian agriculture to mean the soil elevations and ridges constructed in the fields, which flank the running water of the Nile during the season of inundation.

mawwal: The term is used to indicate a nonclassical verse form, a folk verse form or a free song with no set tune. Inasmuch as the folk *mawwal* allows for metrical variations and alternating rhymes, it can be extended for narrative purposes and is often used to tell the stories of folk heroes.

mim: The name of the twenty-fourth letter of the Arabic alphabet; sounds like the letter *m*.

omphalos: The Greek term for navel which indicates not only a body part but also the centrality of being.

qasida: The classical verse form in Arabic poetry often rendered as ode in English translation. It is characterized by monorhyme and by the use of one of the sixteen classical meters. It usually opens up with an erotic prelude and a lament over the ruins of the beloved's encampment and then proceeds to its intended theme: panegyric, satire, et cetera. The term is used in modern literary discourse to mean simply a "poem."

ra': The name of the tenth letter of the Arabic alphabet; sounds like the letter *r*.

rabab: A string instrument known in English as rebec. In Egypt it has one or two strings and is used in folk music, especially accompanying a bard narrating folk epics or singing *mawwals*.

rajaz: One of the classical Arabic meters known as a folk meter in pre-Islamic Arabia for its simplicity.

shadoof: An irrigation sweep used to lift water, formerly common in Egypt.

sirwal: Baggy trousers traditionally worn by Oriental women, known in fashion jargon as "harem pants."

sura: One of the 114 chapters of the Koran.

ta':   The name of the sixteenth letter of the Arabic alphabet; sounds like the letter *t* stressed.

taqiyya: The disguise and denial of faith that is permitted under compulsion or threat.

tharida: A feastly Bedouin dish of meat, broth, and soaked bread.

ya: An Arabic vocative and exclamatory particle, often preceding formulaic refrains in *mawwals.*

ya':   The name of the twenty-eighth and last letter of the Arabic alphabet. When written, it looks like a sofa or bed.

Explanatory Notes

EARTH JOY

pp. 1–20   "Earth Joy" is one of four sets of poems in the *Quartet of Joy*, each named after one of the four elements considered to be the constituent parts of the physical universe in ancient Greek philosophy, as well as in Arab-Islamic and European medieval thought. These elements (earth, fire, water, air) were considered capable of changing into each other when sharing a common quality (that of cold, hot, dry, or wet). The physics of this doctrine, developed by pre-Socratic philosophers, correspond to the psychophysiological doctrine of the four humors based on the teachings of the Greek physician Galen (129–199 A.D.), who believed that body fluids (blood, choler, phlegm, melancholy) needed to be held in a state of equilibrium. Both doctrines were dominant until the seventeenth century, marking literature and science of the time. Matar charges these essential elements with symbolic power.

     "Earth Joy" is made up of six poems, written between 1975 and 1987. They are variations on the poet's wonder at, and love for, the earth. The first three poems are a prelude in different keys: they initiate the reader into the poetic logic, diction, and themes of the divan. The last three poems involve a beloved, a father, and a son, respectively—all of which are poetic masks for the earth.

First Prelude

p. 1   "First Prelude" was written in 1975, when the poet was forty years old. The poetic persona makes repetitive references to the age of forty, expressed in the figure of "forty doors." Reaching forty has symbolic value in Arab-Islamic culture. It is the age when Prophet Muhammad received the Revelation, and has come to be seen as the age of fulfillment. The poetic persona at the end of the poem awaits the moment of completion and the turning point in his life—bringing forth the Poem.

p. 2, lines 9–10	The italicized word *fasila* (Arabic plural: *fawasil*) refers specifically to Koranic rhymes (*see* Glossary); the "rhythm-beads" refer to the prayer beads or rosaries used to repeat formulaic verses or invocations in supplication.

Second Prelude

pp. 2–5	"Second Prelude" was written in 1975 and emphasizes, as in "First Prelude," the age of forty, using the locution of "forty doors," which has become by now a signature of Matar.
p. 2, lines 19–25	Zeno of Elea, the Greek philosopher (born c. 490 B.C.), is known for his paradoxes used to refute notions of plurality and motion. The two paradoxes referred to here are based on what is called in logic an argument of *reductio ad absurdum*. Inasmuch as Achilles gives the tortoise a head start, he can never catch up with it, according to Zeno; for in overtaking it, he has first to get to its preceeding point, and by the time he gets there, the tortoise will have moved to a farther point, and when Achilles tries again to reach that new point of the tortoise, it will have moved yet farther, and this goes on indefinitely to show how the swift Achilles can never catch up with the slow-moving tortoise in their race. The paradox of the arrow argues that objects at rest occupy a space equal to their dimensions; and since a flying arrow at any moment is occupying a place no more or less than its dimensions, it follows that the moving arrow is at rest.
p. 2, lines 26–27	Muhammad ibn 'Abd al-Jabbar al-Niffari was an Islamic mystic who lived in Iraq and Egypt in the tenth century. His scattered writings, composed in Niffar (his home town) and on the Nile, were collected by one of his descendents. He is known for two books, *Mawakif* and *Mukhatabat*, and other fragments which have all been edited and translated into English by A. J. Arberry (Cambridge University Press, 1935). Both works are made up of fragments of Sufi teachings in aphoristic style, in what has come to be seen as a medieval Arabic form of the prose poem. Al-Niffari was influenced by al-Hallaj, the martyred Sufi, and in his turn, al-Niffari influenced the Andalusian mystic Ibn 'Arabi (1165–1240). Al-Niffari is known in the history of Sufism by the notion of *waqfa* ("stay" or arresting contemplation). *Waqfa* is a mystic state higher than *ma'rifa* (knowledge), and transcending the condition of humanity; it allows the mystic to partake in a vision of God. The "rose" referred to here alludes to

the mystic flower that al-Shibli (born in Baghdad in 861, becoming an ascetic at the age of forty) threw to the crucified martyr and mystic Al-Hallaj (858–922) as a token of the inexpressible Sufi passion.

p. 3, lines 11–13   In Islamic literatures, wine drinking, with all its para-phernalia of glasses, tables, and tavern keepers, was used as motif for wine songs, known as *khamriyyat* (derived from the Arabic word for wine, *khamr*). But it was also used in mystic poetry, in a metaphoric and symbolic sense, indicating the intoxication of the soul with divine love.

p. 3, line 15   The expression "salted grass" indicates grass treated so as to conserve its freshness. The grass is "mummi-fied," so to speak, as Matar puts it in Arabic.

pp. 3–4   Matar's poetry abounds in references to flora and fauna of his Delta region in Lower Egypt. Here he names plants that grow near the Nile River and its canals.

p. 4, lines 6–35   The poetic persona is addressing the earth personi-fied as a woman—not a mother-earth, but rather a seductress-earth—with the metaphor of the female body extending and branching out.

p. 4, line 25   *Omphalos* is the Greek word for navel, which carries in its Greek form (as used by Homer and reused by Joyce) the notion of centrality of being. In Arab-Islamic civi-lization, Arab geographers called Mecca—and some-times Baghdad—the navel of the earth.

p. 4, line 35   This alludes to the Islamic accounts of creation as found in exegetical works and popular lore: God ordered three angels, Gabriel, Michael, and Asrafil, one by one, to take from the seven layers of the earth seven handfuls of sand; but the earth would not grant them this. When 'Azra'il, the angel of death, received the divine order, he took from the earth, by force, a quantity of sand enough to create the first human being. God then ordered rain to pour down in order to soften the clay; then the angels kneaded it, and finally God made the mold and left it to dry before animating it.

p. 5   The poetic persona depicts here a young girl learning how to read and write. The letters *alif* and *ya'* are the first and the last in the Arabic alphabet, corresponding to the Greek *alpha* and *omega*. The pair has been used at times to refer to Christ who had said, according to John the Divine, "I am Alpha and Omega, the begin-ning and the ending" (Revelation 1:8). These child-like writings by the little girl are depicted in the poem as acts of creation. The connection between the letter and the divine exists also in Islam where the Koran is considered the miracle of Islam because of its sublime and incomparable verbal perfection.

p. 5, lines 13–18   The one and four written by the young girl are Indian numerals, as commonly used in computing in the Arab world (in contrast to Arabic numerals used commonly in the West), and it is the number in its iconic form that the poetic persona refers to. Thus, one—in Indian numerals—looks like a singular vertical line while the four looks like a two-story house.

p. 5, lines 23–26   The allusion is to the Koran VI:95, "It is God who splits the grain and the date-stone, brings forth the living from the dead; He brings forth the dead too from the living." All translations of Koranic citations in the notes and in the body of the poems consistently draw on A. J. Arberry's sensitive rendering of the Koran in English. The decision to use an already established and prestigious rendition of the Koran is based on the expectation that this English text of reference will capture the intertextual effect that the poem triggers in Arab readers, as they sense the different ways that the poem incorporates or points to the Koran.

p. 5, lines 27–29   The allusion is to Christ's miracle of multiplying loaves and fishes to feed the multitude. *See* Matthew 14:15–21; 15:32–38.

Third Prelude

pp. 6–8   "Third Prelude," a hymn to the earth from which men and women are made, was written in 1984. Koranic allusion and references abound here, especially to the creation of humans from earthen clay. *See* the Koran XV:26.

p. 7. lines 22–29   The covenants of the Unknown and the Adamic covenant refer to covenants between God and human-kind as represented by Adam—who was shown the generations to come of men and women. *See* the Koran VII:172–173, "And when thy Lord took from the Children of Adam, from their loins, their seed, and made them testify touching themselves, 'Am I not your Lord?' They said, 'Yes, we testify'—lest you should say on the Day of Resurrection, 'As for us, we were heedless of this,' or lest you say, 'Our fathers were idolaters aforetime, and we were seed after them. What wilt Thou then destroy us for the deeds of the vain-doers?'"

p. 7, line 35	The "guarded tablet" refers to the original copy of the Koran (and the record of divine decisions) as mentioned in the Koran LXXXV:22, "Nay, but it is a glorious Koran, in a guarded tablet."
p. 8, line 1	"Certitude" *(yaqin)* is a Koranic concept and is referred to in more than one place, as in "Surely this is the truth of certainty" (LVI:95) or "and we cried lies to the Day of Doom, till the Certain came to us" (LXXIV:47), but here in the poem it evokes "Proclaim thy Lord's praise, and be of those that bow, and serve thy Lord, until the Certain comes to you" (XV:99).
p. 8, line 2	The Koran refers to the Trumpet of the Day of Judgment in ten different places (VI:73; XVIII:99; XX:102; XXVII:87; XXXVI:51; XXXIX:68; L:20; LXIX:13; LXXVIII:18); the allusion here is to the Koran LXXIV:47, "For when the Trumpet is blown, that day there shall be no kinship any more between them, neither will they question one another."

Some Time before Some Death

pp. 8–17	The poem was written in 1987, using the classical persona of the warrior poet to depict a contemporary predicament.
p. 10, lines 2–9	The allusion is to Noah's dove. *See* Genesis 6–9 and the Koran VII:59–64; X:71–73; XI:25–49; XXVI:105–22; LXXI:1–28; and XXIII:23–31.
p. 11, lines 10–29	The poetic persona describes scenes carved on the wall of a pharaonic temple.
p. 15, lines 12–13	This alludes to the Koran XXI:30, "Have not the unbelievers then beheld that the heavens and the earth were a mass all sewn up, and then we unstitched them and of water fashioned every living thing?"
p. 15, line 34	This is a reference to the Koran XXI:96, "and they slide down out of every slope."
p. 16, line 18	The eagle here is a symbol of the nation in its many instances. Thus the "last eagle" refers to the last wave of the nation. In Arabian and Semitic lore the eagle was associated with the moon and time and was used as a national symbol. The legends tell of the sage Luqman who had seven eagles: each had a distinct name, but all the names signify progeny or offspring. When his seventh and last eagle started agonizing, Luqman knew his final hour had arrived and he broke into elegiac verse mourning his own death.

The Visit

pp. 17–18   This poem, written in 1984, is a dirge recited by the poetic persona in his ritual visit to his father's grave.

Earth-Rejoicing Lad

pp. 19–20   The poem, written in 1978, is dedicated to the poet's son Loay.

p. 19, line 7   The reference here is to magic spells and divining as mentioned in the Koran CXIII:4, "women who blow on knots."

p. 20, line 30   The reference here is to the Koran LXXXVI:7, "he was created of gushing water issuing between the loins and the breast-bones."

FIRE JOY

pp. 21–33   The poem was written between 1975 and 1981 and celebrates fire as an ushering phenomenon in rebirth, resurrection, and rejuvenation. It is made up of three parts.

I.

p. 22, line 31   The Hawk refers to the banners used in early Islamic expeditions which had an emblematic hawk on them.

p. 24, lines 23–32,   The letters *mim, ta'*, and *ra'* constitute the name Matar
p. 25, lines 1–9   in Arabic (which also means "rain"). The poet here is spelling out his own name, with the form of the scripted letters indicating an iconic value, like hieroglyphs.

p. 25, line 12   This refers to the Koran II:223, "Your women are a tillage for you; so come unto your tillage as you wish."

p. 25, lines 13–14   *See* note to p. 20, line 30.

p. 25, line 22   The sycamore is a long-living tree and was considered in Pharaonic Egypt as the symbol of immortality; it is associated with Osiris.

Mawwal *from the Gardens of a Woman*

p. 26, line 1   The refrain *ya layl, ya 'ayn*, which means literally 'Oh night, Oh eye' is used in vocal improvisation in Arabic music and in sung *mawwals*. The refrain is modulated over and over by the singer, conjuring suffering and an endless night. It is said that the choice of the words of the refrain is related to being alone at night and tearfully in love.

Mawwal *of the Distant Gaze*

p. 27   *Mawwals* are usually divided into "red" and "green" —the first dealing with motifs of hardship of life and social injustice, and the second with the joys of love and celebration of life; however, many *mawwals* tend to combine the plaint with a hope, as in this *mawwal*.

The Bard's Mawwal

p. 28   This *mawwal* refers to the tragic story of Hasan, the singing minstrel who fell in love with Na'ima and was killed by her family because of this love.

II.

p. 30, line 7   Divorce or repudiation, in Islam, can be either revoked or is irrevocable, that is, final.

p. 31, line 12   The reference is to the Koran, where Noah is addressing his son, who thought he could take refuge in a mountain during the flood: "Today there is no defender from God's command but for him on whom He has mercy" (XI:43).

WATER JOY

pp. 35–52   The poem is in three parts written between 1975 and 1980. It celebrates water which is the source of life, as mentioned in the Koran XXI:30; *see* note to p. 15, lines 12–13. It is also the element that revives the dead earth, as mentioned more than once in the Koran, for example, "and the water God sends down from heaven therewith reviving the earth after it is dead" (II:164).

The Predicate in Advance

pp. 35–40   This poem was written in 1975. The intention of departure, as well as the oppression leading to such a move and the anticipation of promise and fulfilment, is formed in the thoughts and interior monologues of the poetic persona.

p. 36, line 2   *See* note to p. 25, line 12.

p. 36, line 24	The expression "He stayed me" occurs in the openings of al-Niffari's mystic fragments. *See* note to p. 2, lines 26–27.

Ambiguous Terms

pp. 40–46	This poem was written in 1979 and, like the poem preceding it and the poem following it, uses grammatical and syntactical categories for its title.
p. 41, lines 4–7	The reference is to the many arts of divining and fortunetelling practised by Arab Bedouins, including the decipherment of animal footprints *(qass)* or bird flights *(zajr)*, and the positioning of stars *(tali')* or sand tracks *(qiyafa)*, so as to figure out the (mis)fortune they bring.
p. 41, line 30	This alludes to Zachariah's supplication in the Koran XIV:4–6, "O my Lord, behold the bones within me are feeble and my head is all aflame with hoariness. And in calling on Thee, my Lord, I have never been hitherto unprosperous. And now I fear my kinsfolk after I am gone; and my wife is barren. So give me, from Thee, a kinsman who shall be my inheritor and the inheritor of the House of Jacob, and make him, my Lord, well-pleasing."
p. 42, line 35	This is a reference to the Koran XXII:75, "Feeble indeed alike are the seeker and the sought!"
p. 43, lines 15–20	These lines interweave statements from different Koranic *suras:* "But as for him who is given his book behind his back, he shall call for destruction and he shall roast at a Blaze" (LXXXIV:7–12); "And when they are cast, coupled in fetters, into a narrow place of that Fire, they will call out there for destruction" (XXV:13); and "Faces on that day humbled, labouring, toilworn, roasting at a scorching fire" (LXXXVIII:4).

Subject Deferred

pp. 46–52	This poem was written in 1975, 1979, and 1980. It is made up of three distinct scenes.
p. 46, lines 9–10	This refers to the Koran XLI:53, "We shall show them Our signs in the horizons and in themselves."
p. 47, lines 1 and 6	These refer to the Koran LXXVIII:2, "Of what do they question one another? of the mighty tiding."
p. 47, lines 8–12	This is a citation from the Koran XVI:26.
p. 47, line 14	This refers to the Koran IX:40, "Sorrow not; surely God is with us."

| p. 47, line 23 | This refers to the Koran XXVIII:85, "He who imposed the Recitation upon thee shall surely restore thee to a place of homing." |
| p. 48, lines 9–10 | This is a citation from the Koran IX:42. |

1.

| p. 48, line 21 | *See* note to p. 41, line 30. |
| p. 49, lines 5–15 | These verses are attributed to the eighth-century poet Ja'far al-Harithi. The translation used here is by Herbert Howarth and Ibrahim Shukrallah. *See* the *Anthology of Islamic Literature*, edited by James Kritzeck (Penguin, 1964), pp. 68–69. As before (with Koranic citations), the translators preferred the inclusion of a well-established anthologized version rather than to work out a new translation, in order to evoke the *déjà vu* effect which intertextuality of the original triggers. |

2.

| p. 49 | The notion of poverty is prominent in this part of the poem and recurs in other parts of the *Quartet*. Poverty is esteemed as a noble and liberating virtue among mystics. Suhrawardi, the medieval Sufi, is known for having said: "poverty is my pride." |
| p. 49, lines 28–33 | The scene refers to the device contrived by Yunis, one of the heroes in the Hilali folk epic *(al-sira al-hilaliyya)*. Yunis left his desert encampment during a year of famine to scout for a more promising and fertile land for the nomadic tribe to move to. This part of the narrative is commonly known as "Pioneering" *(Riyada)*. Yunis, however, was captured by the antagonist chief in Tunisia. While a prisoner in the palace, he and 'Aziza—the chief's daughter—fell in love. The lovers contrived a device in order to conceal the situation of Yunis from his tribe, who could figure it out by their fortunetelling art. So as to confuse them, a pool was built in the palace and the lovers would meet on a boat in that pool. Such a scene would necessarily confuse the folk back home and obscure their reading of the situation. The poetic persona in this part of the poem identifies with Yunis because he too (the persona) has been deflected from his quest by a passionate love. The palace is referred to by the poet as a whale, probably because it contains in it Yunis, the Arabic name for Jonah. |

77

pp. 50–51   Here, as in the following poem "Air Joy," dialogues between a male and a female interlocutor take place in dramatic scenes. In Arabic, unlike English, the gender of the addressee is specified in the grammatical construction, thus a reader will be able to tell the male from the female addressee at a glance. The gender specificity of Arabic is lost in English, but to signal it, we preceded the dialogues with dashes; the she-speaker flush left and the he-speaker indented towards the right.

p. 51, lines 4–5   This refers to the Koran XCIII:1–2, "By the white forenoon and the brooding night!"

AIR JOY

pp. 53–64   The poem was written in 1988, celebrating the union of lovers in life and death, with the air and the wind uniting their dust into one.

p. 57, lines 25–33   Yahya ibn Mahmud Al-Wasiti was a thirteenth-century painter from the town of Wasit in Iraq. He is best known for his exquisite illustrations of Hariri's classic Arab work of stylized and ornate narratives entitled *Maqamat* (Assemblies).

p. 61, lines 33–34   This is a reference to the Koran LXXXVI:11, "By heaven of the returning rain, by earth splitting with verdure, surely it is a decisive word."

p. 62, line 36   In Arabic lore, the food cravings of a pregnant woman, if denied, will leave marks and moles on the body of her baby.

On the Poet and the Translators

MUHAMMAD AFIFI MATAR (Egypt) is one of the most distinctive poets in the Arab world today. He was born and brought up in a small village in the Nile Delta, Ramlat al-Anjab (Minufiyya governorate), where he attended the Koranic school, and then went to the adjacent town for formal education. After graduating from the University of Ain Shams at Cairo with a B.A. degree in philosophy, he taught philosophy for many years in Kafr al-Shaykh governorate. There he also founded and edited the influential cultural monthly *Sanabil* (1969–1972), which served as a platform for young and regional talents. He resided in Iraq from 1977 to 1983, where he worked as a literary journalist. For over three decades, he has contributed to major literary journals of the Arab world, including *Al-Adab* (Beirut), *Al-Aqlam* (Baghdad), *Adab wa-Naqd* (Cairo), and *Mawaqif* (Paris). At present, he works as a consulting editor for the General Egyptian Book Organization. Matar has published thirteen volumes of poetry, two books of criticism, and translations of European and Asian poetry. He has been awarded several prizes, including the State Prize (Egypt), Taha Hussein Prize (University of Minya), Poetry International Prize (Netherlands) and Cavafy Prize (Greece). Special issues of literary magazines and poetic reviews have been dedicated to Matar in acknowledgment of his stature and integrity. He has participated in poetry readings and festivals in the Arab world and Europe, the most recent of which was the festival of "Les Belles Etrangères" in France, devoted to foreign literature.

FERIAL GHAZOUL (Iraq) was educated in the Arab world, Europe, and the United States. She is presently a professor of English and comparative literature at the American University in Cairo. She is the editor of *Alif: Journal of Comparative Poetics*, coeditor of *The View from Within: Writers and Critics on Contemporary Arabic Literature*, and author of *Nocturnal Poetics: The Arabian Nights in Comparative Context* and *Saadi Youssef* (in a series on poets and poetry). She has written a number of articles on Matar which have appeared in the *Journal of Arabic Literature, Jusoor, Fusul*, and *Al-Karmel*.

JOHN VERLENDEN (United States) studied English literature at Rhodes College and received his M.F.A. degree in creative writing from Louisiana State University. He presently teaches creative writing at the University of New Orleans; he studied Arabic while teaching English at American University in Cairo. He has published poetry and essays, most regularly in *Exquisite Corpse*. His fiction has appeared in various journals including the *Missouri Review*.

End of English
Translation

End of
Arabic Text

محمد عفيفي مطر

رباعيـــة الفـــرح

شـــعر

قصـــائد الديـــوان

فَرَحٌ بالتراب

مفتتح أول

طلقة الماء الزجاجية برصاصتها الشفافة:
سددها البحر – بين النوم واليقظة –
فأردتني عشقاً،
وغشي عليّ من وهج الظهيرة المبتعدة..

أطرافي مهرة والبحرُ ربيعٌ من ليونة الجسد الذي
يمدُّ لي موائده بالجوع أطباقاً أطباقاً
وأحلامي طيور متوحشة فاجأها الليل بالحيرة
ونداء المسافةِ
أربعون باباً هي مزولة أعضائك المفتوحة على
ينابيع الطعام والشراب
أكلتُ وشربتُ،
نظرت إلى أقدامي فرأيت الخطوة ولم أر الطريق
أربعون باباً أجيئك منها بعدد السنين
أكتسي دماً ولحماً وأتكلم ولا أَولد.

شمس منتصف الليل وقمر الظهيرة:
هل هذا هو اقتران الوطن بالنفي
واللغة بفزع الكهوف؟

هل هو ميقات استطالة الظل أم موعدٌ

لفطرة الينابيع أَزِفَتْ تفجراتُه

لتكتمل أعضائي وتنفرط فواصل ومسابح إيقاعات!

أقول أنا المولود من أربعين امرأة:

هذه بطولة الانتظار وتعثرات الخضرة البطيئة..

١٩٧٥

مفتتح ثان

أربعون باباً .تشتبك منها الدوائر وتتواشج
الدهاليز وتتفرع أشجار الدرج صعودا وهبوطا
يفاجئني صديقي «زينون» الإيلي ويفتح المسافة
بين السهم والأفق
ويملأ فراغ الأوراق بوحشية السباق بيني
وبين سلحفاة البداية وكلمة الفتح.
ويفاجئني صديقي النفري بوردة الماء المدمم ووهج
البحر وطعم الهواء المالح
فأشتهي الخبز وأنتظر الوقت وطفولة المسامرة
والكشف وإيذان الذهول
أنا المولود من أربعين امرأة
أتربص لهذيان التذكر وجموح الأشكال
فالأرض محدودبة على حصاد الموت وقوارير
الظمأ المعتق

فهل أنتَ على أهبة أيها الساقي
لتفتض أختام الطين وتمد المائدة بالكؤوس
وشظايا الطعام وأحزمة العشب المحنط والزيتون
أم تتلفت كما يتلفت الرأس الساقط من شجرة الجسد!
وهل أنتَ -- بين من مضى ومن يأتي – خليفةٌ
على المسافة بين أول خطاك على حصباء الموت
وأول خطاك على عتبة الزلزلة!
ها هو النهر يجلس القرفصاء
يفك سيور خفيه المجدولين من البرنوفِ
وليونة العشب
عباءته من هشاشة القش وضفائر السنابل

تطرزها أزهار القرطم والزغلنت
وتتدلى من عراها أربطة العليق وأزرار
الرمان الساقطة من وردة الدم السنوي
ها هو يتجلى كائنا نباتيا مزدحم الأعضاء
بالطحلب والبشنين ورغوة الخضرة والرائحة الميتة
والليل يساقط من أطراف الأيدي
وبين الأصابع تتلاصق الأحجار بيوتا مغلقةَ
النوافذ ومجهولة الدهاليز.
فهل أنتِ امرأة لأن الملوك يزدحمون بين القميص
وبين تضاريس الجسد؟
أم أن الملوك يحاصرونك لأنك امرأة؟
أم أنتِ امرأة لأن نهديك وفخذيك مقاصيرُ
للشجر المكتوب على أكف الليل والنهار ودوامات الريح؟
كشف الليل عن ساقيك وانتصب عمود الصبح
بين نهديك أرض ممدودة ليوم موعود
وهذا قران العناصر
تساقط عنكِ دريئة الحطبِ والشجرِ اليابسِ
وتعلو شجرة الأفق
والنحل البري يبني سداسياته في صحن السرة الناضجة
فيسلكون حولكِ مسالكَ الريح صفاً صفاً كأن
على رؤوسهم الطير
ذلك أوانُ الفرح والموت
وأنت من كل شيء ينبوعُ ينتفض بالحمّى
وصرخةٌ تقرفر في دمها
تلك آية لمشيئة الغضب وقيامة الأرض السابعة
فانظري..
ها هي الشمس مقطوفةٌ من براعمها

نثرت من قطيفتها زَغَباً فوق برج الولادةِ

تكتبين الألف خطوة ساقطة كالقذيفةِ

على لحم الورق المستسلم

وتكتبين الياء سريراً يترجرج على زئبق اللغة.

تتعلمين الأرقام والحساب:

هذا هو الواحدُ..ملتفٌ بالفرادةِ،

منتشرٌ وكثير

ترسمين الأربعة بيتا من طابقين مفتوحا للرياح والمطر

تجمعين فتحبل الكائناتُ باحتفاليةِ الزواج

تطرحين فينسلخ النهار من الليل وينفلق النوى

ويخرج الحيُّ من الميت

تقسمين فتمتلىء السلال سمكاً وأرغفةً

تقفين على عتبة الألوان وإغراءات المساحة

والأقلام شجرةٌ مقطوعةٌ من قوس قزح

يسكنها النوم المجنون بالصور

وتعشش فيها طيور الحلم والرغبة

تتقدمين خطوةً إلى أبهاء الشكل وأروقة العبارةِ

فينقلب كل شيء

ينقلب كل شيءٍ..

١٩٧٥

مفتتح ثالث

هل قلتُ أن الأرضَ أقربُ من دمي،
أن الدمَ الفوارَ طميٌ من خرائطها
ومشويٌ من القرميد يدفُقُ بالسلالات القديمة
والرفات من الخرائبْ؟
قلتُ صلصالٌ وفخارٌ هو الدمع المبادرُ والمقيمْ؟

قلتُ البلادُ قريبةٌ ليست تمرُّ الشمسُ مَن دوني
ولا ترمي الرياح عباءة الغيم الرحيمْ
إلا وكنتُ تَشَقُّقَ الألوان في شفق انهمار الفجرِ
والإيقاعَ في الأمطارِ،
ليست مولجاتُ النوم في الرؤيا وليل الخلقِ
في صبح السديمْ
إلا خطاي الباحثاتِ عن البلاد المستكنَّة في البلادْ..

قلتُ البلادُ قريبةٌ..فيداي منسربٌ لمحض اللمسِ
فوق خلائق الملكوت فيها بين طلع شهوةٍ
متوقد الودق العميمْ
- فالريح حبلى والدم اللونيّ معقودٌ سلالاتٍ
وأنساباً تواشجُ خفقةَ الطين المقدّسِ -
وانفجار الأرض بالميلاد
بين الماء والجذر القديمْ
فالأرض أرخت ظلها المكدود من طمثٍ وخلقٍ واشتهاءْ
ويداي منسربٌ لمحض اللمسِ..
عشرٌ من نوافير الحواسْ..

هذي هي البطن التي استرخت قباباً ليس

يعروها سوى حُمّى يديَّ، الريحُ إيقاعُ الزيارة

والخطى من لفح أنفاسي

ومشبوبُ الجنون نعومةٌ في سنبل القمح

الخشونةُ في انحدار العشب والوديان مشبوبُ الجنون

وأنا أمد يديَّ

فيما بيننا بحرٌ وصحراءٌ ومشبوبُ الجنونْ

والأرضُ أقربُ من دمي..فأنا اختيار الأرضِ

والأرضُ اختياري، والمواثيقُ التي انعقدتْ

بغيب الذرِّ في الأصلاب يشهد مغزلُ

الأفلاك والفجرُ المرفرفُ تحت عرش الله أن

النطقَ بالإشهاد مختومٌ بوشم دمي وطيني

النطق يشهد أن رقَّ الموثقِ المعقود ما

بيني وبين الرب يفتح أضلعي في لوحه المحفوظِ..

فانطق يا يقيني

وانفخ دمي في الصُّور، ولتشهد يميني

أن المدائنَ والمدافنَ تحت محض اللمس يرجفُ

من رواجفها انفجار المشهد اليومي بالرؤيا..

١٩٨٤

وقتٌ ما لموت ما

للريح محلولُ العباءة أم لوجه الشمس ما
ذَرَّ الترابُ على جبينكَ من نحاس الفجر!
مهرتُكَ استهلَّ صهيلُها ضبحاً
صداه الغيمُ والظلُّ الخفيفُ
على اتساع الأرض والفلوات،
تعلو خطوةَ الشمس التي تعلو كأنَّ المهرةَ اشتبكتْ
بمهماز الفضاء وأنتَ تعلو فوق صهوتها
المطهمة الركاب بنجمة الصبح الأخيرة
ليس للشمس الوليدة في قماط الفجر أن
تَتَشَعَّعَ الحناءُ منها في ذؤابة شعركَ المرخَى: لها مسُّ
الحوافر..دونَها وهج الركاب بنجمة الصبح الأخيرة
ليس لليل المولِّي في سهوب الفجر أن
يلقاك عَدْواً من براريه القديمة: ألف
عامٍ والضحى والليل ينتسخان وجهكَ
لا تضيءَ ولا تذوب ولا تنام ولا تقوم
وأنتَ في ألفية الأرق المنوَّم لستَ تسمعُ
غيرَ نزف الأرض في وَدَق الرواعد بالأسنّة لستَ
تسمع أو ترى إلا تراب سلالة النوم المؤرَّق إذْ
تذرّيه السوافي العاصفاتُ وأنتَ تعقد عقدةَ
الثأر الكظيم وتصطلي حُرَقَ التذكر والحنين..
فهل لمحلول العباءة هذه الريحُ الفتيةُ
أم لوجهكَ من نحاس الفجر ما ذرَّ الترابُ!
ألفٌ من السنوات كانت ألفَ بابْ
يأتيك منها السيل والطوفانُ
يجرف ما انتظرتَ من الأجنة..

أَلِفُ بابْ

تتفتَّق الآفاقُ منها بالهزائم والخرابْ
تجلو بعظمكَ فضةَ الأصفاد
علَّ بجوهر القيدِ الشكيمةَ والركابْ
غالتكَ في العشق النساءُ فهن أطلالٌ من
الفتن الدواثر في نشيج الإغتراب
طَلَعتْ عليكِ جميلةٌ فرعاءُ في وهج الضحى العالي
وأنتَ مطوَّحُ الأعماق ما بين الحضور البور
والخصب الغيابْ
طَلَعتْ وخلفكما سراديبُ الملوك الأقدمين
يضيء فيها من شباب الصخر عشقٌ بازغٌ
قلتَ: انتهى طوفانك السريُّ..هذي من
شظاياكَ القديمة قد أتتكَ حمامةً بيضاءَ تحمل من
جَنى فوضاكَ من غرق القصائد في وحول
الخلق والإلهام غصناً مثمراً..
قلتَ: أَتَّبعْ أهواءَ رقصتها وبعثرْ ما تبقَّى من
بكائكَ أو رمادكَ في غوايات الضحى أو في
غوايات الصواهل من حروف كلامها أو
لثغة الراء المهيِّجة..اتبعْ بهوَ الملوك الأقدمين
إلى أوائل دهشة الإنسان للدنيا وصورة ما
تجلى من ضرام العشق للأرض الوسيعة
والسماوات المضوَّأة القبابْ
قلتَ: اتبعْ رقصَ الغزالة فهي تُغوي في
دمائكَ لهفةَ الشعْر المزلزل والحنينَ الصعبَ..
لا تدري أتُغويكَ القنيصةُ أم هي الصيادُ يرقبُ
بغتةً من غفلة الأنس الرحيم فتدرِّيكَ بما
يشفُّ وتنثني ودماكَ تَشْخُبُ

قلتُ: أَتْبعُها،.. وفي بهو الملوك سيعقدُ

السحرُ المرمَّدُ في السراديب السحيقة عقدةَ

الفرح الخفيَّ فتستجيشُ وأستجيشُ وننتهي للبدءِ..

كانت لمسة الكفين فوق

برودة الأحجار ميثاقَ التذاوب في مشاهدها:

الحياة بفيضها انفرطت على الجدران،

طعم النهر يَقْطُر في العناقيد، الطيور بهية الأسراب

في الأحراش، في المستنقعات الزهرُ والسمكُ الملوَّنُ،

والمجاذيفُ الرشيقة تضرب الإيقاعَ

للموال والرقص المجنَّحِ،

والخلائقِ في زفافٍ من سفاد الطير والحيوان،

جذدٌ يلبسون رشاقة الموت الجليل،

وكان قوس النصر فلاحين عصّارين صيّادين حفّارين.

والملك استراح على أريكة ملكه يسقي مليكته وتسقيه..

العُقابُ محوِّمٌ

بجناحه الذهبِ، التماعة عينه شمسُ تضيءُ

المشهد الحجريَّ..

كانت لبهةُالشعْر القديمة تشرئبّ.

ويستفيضُ بها رمادُكَ

كنتَ تجهشُ بالقصيدة وهي في أصفادها الحجريةِ،

التفتَتْ جوارحُكَ..النداءُ بكل جارحةٍ يغمغمُ،

والتفتَّ وقلتَ: ينبجسُ السرابْ

ماءً عميمَ الرَّوْح والريحان، يطلع من شظايا

الموت والدمن الخرابْ

موّالكَ المصفودُ في ألفية النوم المؤرَّقِ..

يرجفُ الحجرُ، الحياة تعيد سيرتها:

ثغاءُ الطير والحيوان يعلو، الزهر منفتحٌ لأسرابٍ

١٢

الفراش وعاسلات النحل، تبتلّ الشواديفُ،
المياه يفضْنَ بالبشنين والسمك الملوّن،
والمراكب مثقلاتٌ بالبواكير، الجنود على
ثغور الأرض والموت الجليل مرابطون،
الأرض في عرس وقوسُ النصر معقودُ الزخارفِ
والملوك الأقدمون على الأرائك لحظةَ التتويجِ..
ريحٌ من رُخاء السحر
طال بنا اغترابُك، واغترابي في رميم الأرض والروح
استفيقي من شظاياك انهضي منك
القصيدة في رماد القلب توشك أن تبلّ عظامَها
الإيقاعُ في ضرب المجاذيف استهلّ فَرَفْرفي
لنكونَ في قلب الرعيّة وانفجار الماء
والشمس القديمة فوق أطلال الملوك
استنهضي الحلمَ المبدّدَ في رماد العشق وانفرطي
معي لنكونَ فيضاً في
الحياة المستفيضة من جنون الصخرِ..
كانت تستدير الشمس من أفق الضحى العالي
وتجنح للغيابْ
قلتُ: الضحى والليل ينتسخان وجهكَ
فارتكضْ
خلف الغزالة وهي تمعن في ملاعبها اليباب
قلتُ: ارتكض واترك لهذا الصخر موعده المؤجّلَ علّها
ابتدرتكَ بالعشق المؤجّلِ..
كان صمت الليل معقوداً بلاداً في البراحِ
ومستضيئاً بالجراح وكان منكمشاً ببرد الريح
ملتجئاً إلى صمت الملاحم والمواويل الجريحةِ
والنعاس الرطبِ في خشب الرّبابْ

١٣

حتى استفقتَ وقلت:

من أيِّ البلاد – وقد خلت من عاشقيها – جئت

من أيِّ المواعيد انفلتَ فأنت مطلقة السراح غوايةً

للغابرين الهاربين من القصائد وانتظار العشق!

قالت: أنت..كفكف من مجازات الجنون الصعب..

راودتُ القناعَ عن الملامحِ والملامحَ عن تواريخِ

المبدَّد من رماد العشق

وامتدتْ يداها بالحنان المستريب..

الليل والصحراءُ ينبسطان،

والنهر المشرَّدُ في مخادع طينه،

ريحٌ مبللة الضفائر بالندى، والكونُ أنثى من

أصابعها تقطَّرتْ القصائدُ أنجماً تدنو بأوّل ما

يثير الشعرُ من شجن البدايات..

الحريرُ تفتحتْ منه العُرى:

طلعٌ يفوح بما استكنَّ من الروائح والفراشات الغويّة،

نجمتان على كثيبين،

ارتخاءُ الموجة الحرّى، العمودان الرخاميان

من رمل التشهي، وردتان أضاعتا غمازتين فهل هو

الجسدُ المللمُ من شظايا كل فاتنة مضت أم هذه

حالُ التفتّح في الخليقة لحظةَ التكوين والخلق؟

استرابَ حنانُها القَلقُ ابتدرتُ حنانها بالفيض من

دمعِ التلقي المستشفِّ لعارض الشعر المللوَّح

بالقصيدة، قلتُ للخيل العرابْ

نزقُ الغيوم وشهوةُ الرقص المباغت في انفساح

الأرض باللغة الجموح وشهقةِ الشبق المصلصل في

الصهيل وفي الكتابْ

قلتُ: انظري للغيم..كوني مهرة الملكوت وهو

يشكّل اللغة الحميمة في لسانكِ وامنحي لغتي المذوّبَ فيه

من لغةِ مقطرةِ القبائلِ والصهيلِ..

وكنتَ تجهشُ بالقصيدة وهي في

رَتَقِ الغيم فلا تَفتَّقُ..

ليس ينهلُّ السرابْ

إلا بومض زجاجٍ عينيها ولفتتها الفقيرة لانتصاف الليلِ،

كانت تستعيد رمادها وتعيد سيرتها إلى بدَدِ العناصرِ،

من يديكَ تفلتتْ:

للرمل ينسرب الكثيبان اللذان

توهجا بيديك من وعدٍ تقدّرَ للرضاعة،

لاصطخاب البحر موجتُها التي انعقدت بسرتها

وحقويها على برج التفتح للولادة،

للرياح ولاهتراءات الغيوم حريرُها،

للهدم والشفرات كان رخامها يهوي

ومن بين الركام تهبّ سافية التذكرِ:

ها همو من كل حدبٍ ينسلونَ

بكل مشْرعة القواضب والحرابْ

قد أحدقوا بكَ،

لم تكن تدري أهذي من خواتيم القنيصة أم هو

الفتحُ المزلزلُ باكتشاف حُبالة العشق المؤقت!

فانفلتَّ ونجمةُ الصبح الأخيرةُ وحدها في الأفقِ،

مهرتكَ استهلّ صهيلُها في غابر الشعرِ،

ارتختْ في خطفة الحلم الشكيمةُ، وانجلى من

فضة القيد الركابْ

هذا هو السفر المقدَّر..ليس من زمن له أو
من بلادٍ غيرُ ما يعلو به الوجعُ العصيّ ويبتليكَ نداؤه
الدمويّ
أخرُ هذه الفوضى وأولُ ما يقوم من السلالة:
ذلك النسر المحاصرُ.

كنتَ تفتح من جراحك كلما اشتعل الدمُ الموتورُ
واشتجرت سهام القنص في الآفاق واستُعَرَتْ
بأيدي الزاحفين غريزةُ القتل الجماعيّ، الجراحُ
تفتحتْ لحصاد ما يهوي من الصيد المجندل،
والجواءُ خلونَ من عنف الرشاقة وامتلاك
الريح نسراً بعد نسر..ها هو النسر الأخيرُ
محاصرٌ بين المخارم والسحابْ
والأرضُ – بالوجع العصيِّ وبالنزيفِ
من النداءات المزلزلة –
استعادتْ ذكرياتِ الطلق..

مهرتُك استهلَّ صهيلُها في غابر
العشق المكتَّم في القصيدة، أنت تعلو خطوةَ الشمس
التي تعلو..لها مسُّ الحوافر، دونَها وهجُ
الركاب بنجمة الصبح الأخيرة،
ليس من زمن فلا وجهُ الضحى العالي ولا
الليل المخاتل من رعايا وجهكَ النضّاحِ بالرؤيا،
لكَ الملكوت والعرش المنمنمُ
والقصائدُ من نقيع سلالة النسر المرمّد في دمائكَ
و النداءاتُ العصيات، الطبولُ مدمدمات
والسلالةُ من ملوك العشق طلقاً
يستجيش به التراب..

١٩٨٧/٥/١٥

زيارة

طيناً من الطين انجبلتْ ففي دمي المركوزُ من
طبع التراب الحيّ:
فورةٌ لازب، وتخمرُ الخلق البطيءِ،
ووقدة الفخّار في وهج التحوّل، وانتشار الذرْو في
حرية الحلم، انفراطُ مسابح الفوضى حصىً،
وصلابة الفولاذ في حَدَق الحجارة واليواقيت.
انخطفتُ بنشوة الحمّى، الأوابدُ من وحوش
الطير تحملني وتمرقُ..

في حواصلها أعاينُ محنةَ
الملكوت والأرض الفسيحة..
خفقةٌ تعلو ورفرفة تسفُّ، وبابُكَ الفلكُ
المدوّر يا أبي ورتاجُكَ الطيني والقفلُ الحبالةُ والشراكُ،
وهجعةُ الأطيار إن حلّ الظلام – على الشواهد –
فوق صبّارات قبرك، صوتهن بكل معترك الجواءِ
ومجتلى الدم والمنام هو النداءاتُ الخفية من
ترابكَ والمخاطبةُ العصية من ترابي.

صحوٌ هو الفجر المعلق في ثريات القصيدة إذ
أحركُ في ضرام الخضرة الشمسَ التي
صدئتْ على أَقفال بابكَ يا أبي
ناديتُ في طقس الزيارة: كيف أزمنةُ الترابِ
وكيف تنجبل السلالة من ترابي
ناديتُ والفجرُ المشْعشِع تحت أجنحة الغرابِ
يستنفر الطيرَ الأوابد – من مجاثمها البليلة بالتذكر –
للسياحات العليّة في اجتلاء الأرض والدمِ
من بداية بابكَ الطينيِّ حتى
منتهى صوتي المجلجلِ بالخطابِ..

١٩٨٤

صبيُّ الفرحِ بالتراب

إلى لؤي

بوجهك وهْج دمٍ يتكشف فيه النبيون
والخيلُ تصهل تحت انفلاق الوراثة والسلف الصعبِ
عن وقدة تتغير فيها خطى الريحِ:
يعلو الكلام ويخلع أوزانه
يستعيد المراسيم والسجعَ ينبتُ من هَمهمات الكهانة
والنفْث في عُقَد الليف والعشبِ
فالأرض مُحضَرةٌ والسماء مياهُ مقدّرةٌ
والنبيون مستغرقون..

بوجهكَ ألفُ دمٍ والدوارقُ شفافة وأنا
أتقسّم منكَ بلاداً وأنفرطُ الرقصَ والراقصين
أفيض وأعلو سيولاً من الخَلَف المتكثّرِ..
ها جسدي واحدٌ وكثيرٌ،
وها وحشةُ المتوحد أرضٌ تَزَاحَمُ فيها الخلائقُ،
عهدُ أوثِّقه

سفرٌ في التذكر، بيتُ الإقامة
جلجلةُ العصف، مضْغُ الجذور الطرية في الأرض
فَتْحُ الكلام مع الطير والوحش
خصفُ الفروع ومشتبكُ الماء تحت لساني..
تَنَظّرْتُ:

يخشوشن الصوت أو يسقط
الزغبُ الأصفرُ العشقُ يعطيكَ شارات أمجاده
عُشْباً لائذاً بالذراعين
رائحةً يتفتق منها خفيُّ النداءات..

أسمعُ حمحمةً للذكورة والعشق في خَفْقِ نعليكَ
أسمعُ في جسدي رعدة الملكوت وأسمعُ
خَطْوَ الملايين ما بين خطوي وخطوك..

نذرتكَ تقدمةً لاندلاع البراعم في خشب الوقت
فالشمسُ ذائبةٌ تحت خضرة قمصانكَ الطلُّ
مختبىءٌ والحريقُ

املأ الأرضَ بالغابرين من السلف، املأ
بوجهي الملوِّح أرجاز بادية الأهلِ
واتبعْ خُطى الماء بين الغضا والأراكِ
سهيلٌ دليلكَ والفتحُ ميقاتكَ..
اكتمل العرسُ
فانظرْ دمي هَبوةً في فضاءات عشقك:
أنصبُّ بينكما في مياه الدوارق
ألتفُّ في نُكهة الكعكِ..
وانظرْ دمي في لواءٍ من الطير يسكن أفقَ الممالك والبحرِ:
أسكنُ بين الترائب والصلبِ،
أغدو المواريثَ والوارثين..

١٩٧٨/٣/٢٦

فَرَحٌ بالنار

مضت حقبٌ ليس يدري أوائلَها أو خواتيمَها
أحدٌ غيرُ ميراثه من دمٍ ملكيٍّ وفطرتِه في
مغالبة الموتِ بالإرث أو في غلابِ السقوط عن
العرش بالنسل أو بانتشار ملامحه في
السلالة أو بانتقال الشرائعِ والصولجاناتِ في
الخَلَف الوارثين.
وهم – واحداً واحداً – يجلسون على العرش،
يَحْيَوْنَ، آخرُهم مثلُ أوَّلِهم،
فإذا أزفَتْ لحظة الموت ماتوا كأيهمو:
ملكُ الوقتِ يجثو على ركبتيه وحيداً يقلِّب
عينيه في ملكوت الظلام ويسمع أهوالَ
صوتِ السماوات إذ تتفتَّقُ أفلاكُها
وانفساحِ البسيطةِ إذ تتفجَّر أجداثُها عن
دويِّ التواريخ، يسمع ما التطمتْ في دماهُ
وأنفاسِه من دهور الترقُّب والحذر المتوحِّش
وهو يرى كيف فاضت عليه الممالكُ تأكل من
مُلكِه وتراث السلالة حتى تُساكنه جلدَه ودماه،
وكيف يفيضُ فينحسر الآخرون إلى آخر الظنِّ..

حتى إذا اقترب الفجرُ ألقى عباءتَه وانتضى شِكَّةَ
الصيدِ والحربِ، أرخى شكيمةَ مهرته منصتاً
للنداءات مُزَلزلاتٍ يُناوشْنه عن خطاه،
جوارحُه يتلفَّتنَ، شكتُه تتفصَّد من صدأٍ
وارتعادةِ حمّى، وتعروه غاشيةُ الفجر
بالفرح المتفجِّعِ، يُغريه بردُ الندى وانفساحُ
البسيطة بالصمتِ والطيرِ،
تعلو نداءاتُه:
يا زمانَ الولاءِ المبعثرِ كالريحِ هل
عصفتْ بحدودي عواصفُك المستَسِرَّةُ
فالعرشُ مُنغرساتٌ قوائمُه في
المسافة بين الشهيقِ وبين الزفيرِ
أم انحسرَ الواغلون
فمملكتي آخرُ الظنِّ أولُها!

والولاءاتُ..هل فتحتْ في جدالاتها
الأفقَ فانهمرتْ من ثقوب السماوات
ألويةٌ وبنودٌ تزمجر فيها الطواطمُ داميةً!

وعُقابُ السلالة..هل من مسافة
رفرفة غيرُ ما تزفرُ الروح من حسرةٍ،
غيرُ ما حزَّرته الأسنةُ فوق المخَنَّقِ!
صيدٌ أناوشُه في الطِّراد أم الموتُ
ينسج أشراكَ غيلتِه
يا زمان الولا..لا..أَ..أَ..تِ..تي!

ملكُ الوقتِ يأتي – ككل ملوك السلالة – شِكَّتُهُ

تتلامح منها غواياتُه طعنةً طعنةً،
والجراحُ تنزُّ ينابيعُها تحت مِغْفَرِهِ وهو منفرطٌ
تتساكبُ أعضاؤه من سنابك مهرته
فالنجيعُ على الأرض وشمُ الأهلَّة..
أَنتْ طقوسُ المراسيم والدفن:
هذا أنا وارثُ الوقت..لَفْلَفْتُه في الجراحات،
شكَّته كفنٌ وترابُ السلالة والرملُ والطميُ طيبُ الحنوطْ
وأرقَدْتُه جنبَ جدَّيَ..(تنتظم العائلة
صفوفاً من الشهداء تَراصَفُ أجداثُها جدثاً جدثاً)
وابتدأتُ زماني:

أنا صاحبُ العرش والصولجانْ
تَفَرَّدْتُ في الملك..ما من رعايا سوى شبحي
المتفلِّت في الظل والنور، مملكتي الضدُّ، رؤيا
اصطخابٍ من الإحتمالات، مَسٌّ جنونٍ من
الإنتظار المرابط في عاصفِ المدِّ والجزْرِ..

لي امرأةٌ كلَّلَتْ رأسَها الشمسُ وانفتحتْ بين
هالات حنّائها مدنُ اللون وانتثرَتْ حول
سُرَّتها الأنجمُ العالية
وألقتْ قميصين من زُخْرُفِ الطمي:
هذا قميصُ المسافات – في – الضوءِ
تلبسه خطوةُ الطين في برعمٍ يتنفَّسُ في
حجر الإحتمالات، تلبسه الشهواتُ المليئةُ والرَّحمُ المثقلة
خطفتُ عطيَّتها (والعطايا اختطافْ)
وحاصرني وجهها ..فأَنا النهرُ وهي الضفافْ
وبعثرني رقصُها ..فأَنا البرقُ وهي الرياحْ

(ظلُّ العُقاب مرفرفٌ ما بين أجفاني
في عارضٍ يرفَضُّ منه برقُه القاني
فقرأتُ في أطرافه أسماءَ آبائي وعنواني:

ميمٌ: يدٌ مغلولةٌ في طَميها الواري
والزندُ في بازِلْته العاري
أوتادُ نار السِّقْطِ في
كهف البلاد المعتم الهاري

والطاءُ: عنقاءُ انتظارٍ لَبَّثْتها في
زمان القش والأحطاب تأويلاتُ ما
خطَّتْه في رقِّ الوصايا مهرةُ النار

والراءُ: وشمُ السنبك المفطور من
سُهْد الرباط الصعب في ليل الثغور،
القوسُ في الشدِّ، الهلالُ الفضّةُ،
المهمازُ بين الأفق والينبوعِ، دمعٌ
جمرةٌ ما بين أجفاني)

وهذا قميصُ المسافاتِ ‪–‬ في ‪–‬ الليل:
أنت الفضاءُ المقبَّبُ والحرثُ لي،
بيننا كان ماءُ الترائبِ والصلُّب يغلي بأسمائه،
وأنا فوق نهديك دائرتا حمرة تتكحَّلُ،
من جسدي قد منحتُك مملكةً فتجلَّيت:
هذا هو الأفقُ مسجورةٌ في نوافذه الشَّمسُ،
والنومُ جُمَّيْزةٌ والعصافيرُ مسكونةٌ بالشجرْ
وتحت الخطى غيمةٌ، وشرارةُ برقٍ تطايَرُ في
ودَقِ الطَّلْعِ، والنهر مختبىءٌ في زبيبة نهديك،
أذكرَ طينَ الجسور التي كتبَتْها المواويلُ في
راحة النهرِ، أذكرُ....

موَّالٌ من حدائق امرأة

عينْ يا عيني يا ليلي يا ليلْ
أنا الخطى.. وفي دمي الطريقْ
أنا الذي تزرعه الكتابة
في الريح أو تطرحه في القشرْ
منطفئاً وساقطاً في نفسه،
وضارباً جبهتَه في الصخرْ
كي يفتح المجهولُ في مملكة الأشياء
الحائطَ المقام دون وجهه والقبر

ليل يا ليلي يا عيني يا عين
أنا الذي يحمل من مدائن الرعب مفاتحَ الكنوزْ
فتطلعين.. هُوَّةً مليئةً واقفةً في طرقي
وتسقطين في كل خليَّةٍ من جسدي
فأبدأ التَّخارُجَ الأولَ بالسقوط في الرموزْ

يا عيني يا عين يا ليل يا ليلي
في نَفَسيَ لما تزلْ روائحُ الطحلبِ والشرارة
وشهوةُ النسْج على مناسجِ الأسماءْ
أحملُ في أصابعي الخاتمَ من طينتكِ المواَّرة
بالسرِّ والبكارة
إن قلتُ يا أشجار
تفجَّرتْ في الجسد البراعمُ الخضرُ وسقطتْ
في فميَ الأثمارْ
إن قلتُ يا سماءْ
تكوَّرت في فلكِ العينين

٢٤

كواكبُ الظلمة والنهارْ
إن قلتُ يا خليقة
تجسَّدتْ في زهرة النهدين
والزغبِ المشمس رجفةُ المدائن التي
تُولَدُ في توحُّدِ الأنساب والكتابة

يا ليلي يا ليل يا عيني يا عين
أتعبني السُّكْرُ وأثقلتْ ذاكرتي مواسمُ القطافْ
أسندتُ رأسي مثقلاً بالشعرِ والقدرة
أغفيتُ..أعضائي هي الأرضُ الوسيعةُ
والخليقةُ قبضةٌ من طينتي
والناسُ أبنائي
يا ليل

موال النظر من بعيد

يا من سيسمع صوتي كلما نعقَتْ
سودُ الغرابيب في رأْدِ الضحى العالي
أو كلما رفرفَ الديجورُ أو نعبتْ
في المجثمِ البالي
بومٌ تُجاوِبُها في دمنةِ الروح تأويلاتُ أحوالي
يا من سيسمعني

صوتي غزالةُ وشمٍ..في خرائطه
تسري الأراقمُ أحبالاً بأحبالِ
نسجٌ تعنْكبُه الأنواءُ في دأبٍ
والصيدُ آخرُ ما أبقته أطلالي:
جمرُ المواقد مدفونٌ برملتها
والعشقُ هودجُ آلٍ فوق فَدْفَدها
يجري ويلمع في حلِّي وترحالي
يا ليل

٢٦

موال المغني

ناديتُ لو أسمعتُ أو بلَّغتُ..
ما كان امتدادُ النهر في طين الكلامْ
إلا بلاداً من دم الصلصال، والأرضُ
استنامتْ تحت بلّور الظلامْ
فاذّاويت فيه، وأرخت
مُهرةُ الأرغول مشدودَ اللِّجامْ
كان المغني في انفضاض العُرسِ
والسُّمّارِ يبكي عشقَه عاماً فعامْ
عيني ويا ليلي وآهْ

وجهُ البلادِ المبهمُ المفطورُ في الرؤيا
اشتباكُ الطير في عصف الغَمامْ
والنهرُ يعلو..ضفّتاه رحمةٌ من
سابغِ النومِ، السواقي لا تنامْ
إلا على جُرحٍ ونزف يسكن الصلصالَ
والموالَ في خبز الفطامْ
عيني ويا ليلي وآه

أسمعتُ لو بلَّغتُ..كانتْ في جُروف
النهر أشباحٌ، وأعشاشُ اليمامْ
منقوشةٌ بالدمِّ ما بين الخطى والطمي،
فجرٌ من دمٍ في النهر عامْ
دوامةً أرختْ ذراعيْها وثوبيْها
ووجهاً من قماط الموت قامْ
ليلي ويا عيني وآه

٢٧

كان المغني طافياً فوق المياه
يمشي به النهرُ الثقيلُ الخَطْوَ من
أهلٍ إلى أهلٍ ومن عامٍ لعامْ
بلّغتُ..لو ينشقُّ عن وجه البلاد
المبهمِ المفطورِ صلصالُ الكلامْ
عيني ويا ليلي وآه

لمن هذه الأرضُ، هذي البلادُ التي
اقتحمتْها البلادُ وأهوتْ بعنقودها حبَّةً حبَّةً،
هذه الأرضُ والأرضُ تلتمُّ من حولها عُصبةً عُصبةً
والمدى قَنْفَذَتْه الرماحُ،
البلادُ التي انفرطتْ من جراحاتها كالقنيصة
بين آلأكفِّ..لمن!
لبستُ من الرعب دُرَّاعةً، قلتُ حصنُ الكتابة
آخرُ ما يملك الملكُ المتوِّحدُ،
تلتمُّ فيه خيولُ الدم المتحوِّلِ.
كان الزمانَ زمانَ الكلاب التي اغتلمتْ
بالكتابات فانطلقتْ تتهارشُ والجيفةُ الملكيَّةُ
تنحلُّ، والأرضُ أحيتْ ليالي غرائزها بشواءِ
الدم الآدميِّ وهذا النباحُ له ثمنٌ:

١ – يتساقطُ معنى الكلام ويهوي اغتلامُ
الكتابات تبقى المسافاتُ مهجورةً والخيولُ
المخيفةُ تأتي الوجوهُ المخيفةُ تأتي.

٢ – تساقطَ لحمُ المعاجم عن عظْم هيكلها الهشِّ
وانفضحتْ رمَّةُ الفعل في صيغة خشبٍ للتوابيتِ،
والإسم يسكنه زمهريرُ الخُواءِ، الدلالاتُ في
بائنٍ من طلاق الإشارة والحسِّ، يستبدلُ
النحْوُ أركانَه، ثم يبقى الكلامُ مسافةَ رملٍ
تُعسكرُ فيها الدُمى والجيوشُ الغريبة.

٣- إذا انفسحتْ في الكتابات نافذةُ الأفق بين
التقيَّة والسرِّ، بين القناع وديمومة الرمز..
فلتكبُري في ظلام الكوابيس أيتها الشمسُ،
ولتنسجي عقدةَ الدم يا رجفةً للمخاض المباغت
يا رجفةَ الرَّحم الواعدة.

٤- وكانت بلادُ الطواغيت سجادةً تتقصَّفُ فيها
رسومُ الشجرْ

وتُطوى أمام المغيرين..
تُطوى..فتعلو عمائرُها..
تتمطَّى بلادُ من الرمل والريحِ..
كان المغني يغني: امنحوا وجهَ هذا الحجرْ
قداسةَ خُطُواتكم واخرجوا..
واكتبوا وطناً يتفتَّقُ كالجرح.

كان الكلامُ
وكان المماليكُ يقتسمون رغيفَ النُّخاسةِ
يرتدُ وحشُ الكلام
خطوطاً من الموت مكتوبةً في جبيني
يُقلِّبُها البرقُ والرعدُ
حتى مخاض الحريق المفاجىءْ.

٥- هو الماءُ يشتعلُ الآن في النهر..كيفَ
النَّجاءُ لكم أيها السابحون مع الماء أو ضدَّه
والمراكبُ تهوي مفكَّكةً "ليس من عاصمٍ"
والخطى غرقُ
والمسافةُ بيني وبين بلادي وعرشي
دمُ وتماسيحُ نارٍ!

خطوةُ الشمسِ أوسعُ من ملكوت الفجيعة،

أعمقُ من قشرةِ الصدأ المتكثّف فوق رغيف البسيطة،

أبعدْ من آخرِ الظنِّ، أقربُ من نَفَس الرئتينْ.

أرى خطوةَ الشمسِ..والأرضُ مهمازُها والرياحُ

الطليقةُ مهرتُها،

فاضربي يا شموسَ الكوابيس في خشب العرشِ

ولْيَسْرَحِ السوسُ فالأرضُ بوابةٌ والردى في

البلاد الطريقْ،

الحريقُ المفاجيءُ دوامةٌ تتمدُّد في أفق الإحتمالات،

والشمسُ تسرعُ.. كانتْ تفرُّ الأقاليمُ من تحتها

تتداخلُ مخطوطةُ الرمل في أحرُف الماءِ

والورقُ المتطايرُ يلتمُّ في مصحف الخلقِ

والشمسُ تسرعُ أبعدَ منا وأقربَ

والوقتُ يرفع نيرانَه الفوضويَّةَ، يحملُ آياتِ

غربتِه وطناً للولادات والإحتمالات..

والشمسُ تسرعُ أبعدَ منا وأقربْ..

أهاربةٌ أنت عريانةً تحت قشر المسافة
أم أنت طالعةٌ مثلما يطلُعُ النهدُ مستورةً؟
أنت تاجٌ من القشِّ يلبسُه ملكُ الوقت منتظراً
لحظةَ البرق خَطْفَ الحريقَ المفاجئِ؟
أم أنتِ قافيةٌ تتوقَّدُ تحت رمادِ الكلامِ؟

وهذي المسافاتُ سروالُك المتفتِّقُ ينغلُ من
تحته الخلقُ يكسو عظامَ دفائنه اللحمُ،
أم أنتِ عصفورةٌ تتنقَّل جمرتُها في غصون الحواسِّ
وتفتح في خشب الإرث بابَ الغمام فتصهلُ
خيلُ الينابيع في جسد الأرض؟
واحدةٌ أنت والكونُ أسماءُ وجهك أم أنت
جميزةٌ في فضاء الخليقة أوراقُكَ الخضرُ طعمُ البلادِ
وظلُّك بيتُ الزواج المقدَّس، في جذْرِكِ
الحيِّ يزدحمُ الماءُ والطميُّ؟

قومي سطوعَ القيامة، واصّاعدي من دمي.. أنتِ يا
شهقةَ الإحتمال المفاجئِ يا فرحَ الأسئلة
فهذي عصافيرُ جمرك مكتوبةٌ
(قفصٌ كل شيءٍ وأفقٌ يُفَتِّحْه الحلمُ)
نائمةٌ أنت مصفودةٌ والضفائرُ معقودةٌ،
بين ثدييك يسَّاقط النومُ، والماءُ والطميُّ فرشُكِ،
والريحُ مكتوبةٌ في صراخ المواويلِ..
قومي اصعدي من دمي..
أنتِ نائمةٌ حول حقوْيكِ يلتفُّ

عقدُ القُرى والمدائنِ..أنت ممدَّدةُ
(كلُّ شيءٍ سريرُ وعاصفةٌ تفركُ العينَ بعد النعاسِ)
ووجهُك أروقةٌ في خراب الممالك..
هذا أنا ملكُ الوقتِ.. تلتمَّ فوق بساطي الخليقةُ،
أدخل في كل بيتٍ، وفي كل بيتٍ رعايايَ،
ألبسُ طميَ القرى خاتماً ولساناً لسطوة قلبي ومَدْرَجَةً
لبلادي التي سوف تشهدُ:
هذا هو الصولجانُ الذي
يغزل الريحَ والبرَّ والبحرَ..
فلتأكلوا ما زرعتم،
أقيموا ولائمَ عهدي..فهذي هي النارَ تَرْفَضُ أثوابُها
وتمدُّ خطاها على فرح الأسئلة
فتمنحها شكلَها في مرايا البلاد..

١٩٨١/١٩٧٥

فَرَحٌ بالماء

١- فصل الخبر المقدَّم

ألتفُّ بالشمس وغبار المسافات المفتوحة
أغسل جسدي بالقش ورغوة الغضب
وخناجر العشب المسنَّنة
وأفتضُّ أختامَ الريح وكمونَ الندى في البراعم.
يسكن النحلُ تحت إبطيَّ وبين أصابعي تختبىءُ
الينابيع الخائفة
والأرضُ زجاجةٌ تهشِّم ألوانَ الطيف وتُذَرِّيها على
جسدي المعلَّق بين الجوع والربيع
أمتلىء شيئاً فشيئاً كاليقطين العسليِّ الأحمر المدلَّى
فوق أهرامات التراب ومصاطب التحاريق
أنضج بطيئاً

ب
ط
ي
ء
أ

وأفرح بمراهقتي واكتشاف دمي
أتجلَّى للأطفال كرةً أرضيةً لامعةً تتدحرج
وللطاغية مؤامرةً ملغومةً تسعى

وللأحْلاس الغاوين لغزاً مطارداً
وأنت تحت عيني حرثٌ يتكوَّر ويتجوَّفُ
لنا المشيئةُ حيث نشاء
وبين السُّرَّتين رغيفٌ ينتظر الوارثين.
وهذا هو الماءُ والماءُ والماءُ
والماءُ بوّابةٌ يفتح الليلُ أقفالها فتمرّ الخلائقُ:
هذي مخاصرةُ البحر للبحر،
هذا زواجُ الينابيع، والنهرُ يسحب مَحْرَمَةَ
العرس منقوشةً بالدنانير والعشب. ينثرُ أقراطَه
وأساورَه،
الماء بوابةٌ يفتح الصبحُ أقفالَها:
ها هو اللهُ يلقي تحيّاته شجراً
وحروفاً يُطَيِّرُها في فضاءِ الكتابة
صفوفاً صفوفاً..

خلعْتُ قميصَ دمي.. اشْتبكَتْ

من حبائل أسمائه لحظةُ الصيد،
أوقفني في مفاجأة السنبلة
لأستألفَ الطيرَ، يُخْتَدَعُ الطيرُ لي:
إهبطي في سلام الغيوم البطيئة.. فلْتهبطي
فَرَحُ القلب أعْقِدُه سنبلاً سنبلاً..
هذه لحظةُ الصيد:

سربُ الحمائم يدخل أبراجَ ذاكرتي،
كلُّ ورقاءَ من نعمة الحرف تجدلُ عشَّ الكلام.
هو الطير.

هذا هو البحرُ محتشدُ النوم تحت الملاءاتِ
والخضرة المعتمة
تلاعبُه في سرير التذكر شمسُ الكوابيسِ والوقتِ،
معْصَمُه ازدانَ بالأرض أَسْوِرةً
والبلادُ الفسيحةُ مرسومةٌ في مدارجه:

ها هي الأرضُ..زهْرِيَّةٌ من رماد الهشاشة
منقوشةٌ بالجعارينِ والخيل، مكتوبةٌ
في شظايا العروشِ «النواويسِ» أسماءُ من
ملكوا صولجاناتها،
فوق فخّارِها المتكسّرِ ما زالت القبلاتُ القديمةُ دافئةً
والخطى فوق وجه الجرانيت تصرخُ
بين حطام العواميد والبهو آلهةٌ تتكلمُ في
كتب الصلواتِ..استمعْ:
ها هو البحرُ يلبس أَسْوِرةَ الأرض
يخلعُها، والنساءُ الجميلاتُ في جسد البحر يفتحْنَ
لي طرقَ اللحظة الملكيّة خضراءَ معتمةً أو
مشجَّرةً بالحرير الرماديِّ والحمرة القانية
سماءُ الظهيرة مثقوبةٌ،
ذَهَبُ الكون يهوي إلى الماءِ، والبحرُ يفتح
قُفْلَ خزائنهِ:

ذهبٌ صاعدٌ
ذهبٌ هابطٌ
والقبابُ على حافة الماءِ تخلع قمصانَ شهوتِها الهاربة
وتُطلق صرختها.

–: راحلٌ أنتَ والذهبُ المتوحشُ في

لحظة المدِّ يبني المدائنَ يحشدُ في الماء
قطعانَه المعدنيةَ، يبني على الماء أبراجَه
والحمائمُ يسقطْنَ من أفقِ الموت؟
أم أنتَ تغسلُ قمصانَ صوتِك في كتب
الماءِ تنتظر البحرَ تمشي على وجهه وتُوَاخي – على
صرخةِ الوقتِ والمدن

المستفيقة للموت – بين النجيلِ المرابط في
قدميك وبين المسافةِ وهي تمدُّ طنافسَها وترجُّ
على القاع مملكةَ النومِ واللغةَ العذبةَ الجامحة؟

–: خلعتُ قميصَ دمي..كلُّ ما فيه أسماءُ نخلٍ
من الغربةِ المستفيضة بين الأكفِّ وبين
العيون القريبة في الهمس، أفعالُ موتٍ
مُقَنَّعَةٌ برماد الهشاشة..

أرحلُ..
هذا هو الرقصُ..أنظرُهُ جسداً يتفرَّعُ
إيقاعُه في الفَراهَةِ والعنفِ..
ها جسدي يتفكَّكُ في الدهشة المستريبةِ،
صَيَّرني الماءُ ماءً وألبستُه صرختي..
جسدي جسدُ البحرِ..ما بيننا وردةٌ حيةٌ تتفتَّحُ
تُغوي دمي بائتلاف الردى والفحولة..

وأرحلُ..والبحرُ عاصمتي وخُطايَ،
أشاركه شهواتِ التنقُّل في جسد الأرضِ..
هل تفتحُ المدنُ المستفيقةُ للموت أبوابَها
للبريدِ المسافرِ بيني وبين القبائلِ بالكتب الجارحة؟

بطيئاً أساورها بين قيلولة الهاجرة
وبين الضِّباع المُطيفة في الحلم.
ماءٌ،

وهذا هو العرشُ..

هذا كرسيُّ الإنسانِ ممدودٌ بين مخاضَتَيْ الوطَنِ الواسعِ،
مسقوفٌ بشَمْلة الليل المرتخية وعواميدِ النهار المليءِ
بتغيُّرات الظلِّ والنور
هذا كرسيُّ الإنسان..تعشِّشُ في مُخَرَّماته إلى
يوم الوعدِ يمامةٌ خضراءُ مُحَجَّلَةٌ مؤتلقةٌ بالأمومة
أكلمها وتكلمني
تُطيفُ على وجه الماء

فأَنْظُرُ:
سيدةٌ يتكشَّف عنها الزَبَدُ ويتفتَّح المحارُ.
هوت نجمةٌ فاستضاءتْ ممالكُها السبعُ،
وانتفضتْ ناقةُ الماء منسوجةً بالعروق المضيئة،
مرَّ سحابٌ كثيرٌ وفي الأرض أعجازُ نخلٍ على هيئة
الآدميين مصفوفةٌ في ممالكها،
الغيمْ يرمي قناديلَه من فُتوق الظلام السماويِّ،
ينكشفُ الرملُ في خفَّة الحلم:
سيدةٌ يتطاير بين ضفائرها سمكُ البرقِ والماءِ،

ينكسرُ الأفقُ تحت خُطاها ..فتهبط،
في الأرض أعجازُ نخلٍ على هيئة الآدميين
تهبطُ سيدةُ الماءِ والبرق..

−: مِنْ أيِّ طينٍ شَوَتْه المقاديرُ فخّارةً، أيِّ آنية
أنتِ منها تَنَضَّحْتِ ناراً مبلّلةً وترشَّحتِ عضواً

فعضوا

وقَلَّبْتِ بين يديَّ جنائنك السبعَ وانعقدتْ في
سريري براعمُكِ اللهبيةَ حتى استوينا قِطافاً دماً؟

١٩٧٥

٢- فصلُ الأركانِ الملتبسة

للقبيلة نارٌ مرمَّدةُ..
ليس من جوهر النار إلا دمٌ جمرةٌ في رماد التذكُّرِ،
طقسُ القرى وشميمُ الثريدةِ والبُنِّ والهيْلِ صلصلةٌ
في بقايا القصيدةِ،

نومُ النساء تَخَطَّفَه فزعُ الحلم
كانت سماءٌ زجاجيةٌ وغرابيبُ سودٌ تُدَوِّمُ
كالعصف..كانت تدقُّ السماءَ فتثقبُها
والشظايا المَدمَاةُ تهوي ومن تحتها الطيرُ
والخيلُ أعناقها تتطايرُ
والنزفُ يعلو ويعلو..فيفتحنَ من صرخة الرؤية الجفنَ:
أرضُ مدى يتشقَّقُ من ظمأً طالَ موسمُه،
والشموسُ الخفيضةُ ترمي الجريدَ المسفَّعَ،
والعشبُ رملُ تذريبٍ بين المضاربِ لافحةُ الريحِ..
خيمةُ شَعرٍ تداولها الخرْقُ والرَّتْقُ،
شمسُ الرَّمادة ذائبةٌ في احمرارِ العيونِ ابيضاضِ
الشفاه المملَّحة،
انتبذَ الأهلُ من وقْدة الصهدِ رملَ الجحيمِ يُديرون
أرغفةَ اللغْو بينهمو يأكلون الأحاديثَ تأكل
أكبادَهم لهجاتُ التذكر، أيديهمو تَتَلَقَّطُ جَمرَ الحصى،
ويخُطّون في الرمل يستقرئون الطوالعَ والقصَّ
يستنهضون العرافات إرثَ القَيافةِ والزجرْ،
والشمسُ تدنو جمالُها اللهبيَّةُ..
هم حمّلوني شموساً تذيبُ اليرابيعَ والضبَّ..
راحلتي ظمأً كدَّسته التواريخُ جوعٌ يؤاكلني جسدي..

٤.

وأنا من زمان القبيلةِ أصطحبُ الغولَ أسمعُ
زمزمةً لاغتلام السِّعالي مع الجنِّ
أحملُ سَجْعَ الأَليَّةِ والموثِقِ الصعبِ،
والنهرُ وجهُ الطريدةِ بين سراب السباسبِ.

غلبني الحالُ واعتوَرتني وارداتُ الحواسِّ
وعوارضُ المشاهدةِ،
وكتابُ الأرض يتقلَّبُ بين التأويلِ
فأَلملمُ من صدى الحروف قائمَ الأمرِ وفسحةَ البصيرةِ..
للبلاد أطرافٌ مبلَّةٌ يغمرُها الماءُ:
جدائلُ محلولةٌ في البحر تترسَّبُ عليها
بلُّورات الملحِ الفضِّيِّ فيشتعلُ الرأسُ شَيباً
والطمثُ لما ينقطعْ
أقدامٌ مرتخيةٌ تتناسلُ بين أصابعها السراطينُ
والكائناتُ الهلاميَّةُ والصدَفيَّةُ
وغِراء الزواحف المتسافدَةِ والأعشابُ المتوهِّجةِ..
وبينها وبين الخطوةِ مسافةُ دمٍ لا يجيءْ.
فمٌ يتقَرَّحُ في شفتيه خُرَّاجُ الكلامِ وتعشِّشُ
الطيورُ بين أسنانه المفَلَّجةِ. وينمو الطحلبُ
والنخلُ على بقايا الفرائسِ
وبينه وبين البلاغ مسافةُ صرخةٍ مُطفأةٍ في
الذاكرةِ لا تعلو.
يدان معقودتا الأصابع تتساقطُ منهما الحنَّاءُ
ويَقطُرُ الدهنُ،
فتشتعلُ غرائزُ القرْش وتشتبكُ الحيتانُ حول
الفلَذات المتفتِّتة المصبوغة بالعنْدَم والعُنّابِ.
وللبلاد شكلُ الجسد المسَجَّى الذي يحمله

قَتَبٌ من معجون النفط ورَميم السلالات
المتخمِّرة وغائط الكَلْبيَّين
تَسْمَلُ الشمسُ عينيه:
أوَليسَ من ماءٍ بل أليسَ من وهْم الفرحِ به بل
أليس من وهْم وجوده في قيعةٍ هنا أو هناك!
بل ماءٌ وجسدٌ نَقيعٌ لا يغرق ولا يشرب
هلكَ الطالبُ والمطلوبْ..

تَخَطَّفني الجندُ..
قصرُ أبيكِ على النهر:
أعمدةٌ مرمرٌ يتعرَّقُ فيه تداخُلُ لونٍ بلونٍ
وصوتُ الخطى زَجَلٌ تتعالى القبابُ به
والسماواتُ معْصورةٌ تتقطَّر بين الثريّاتِ
نهرٌ وشمسٌ أسيران في السقف؟
قلتُ: انتهيتُ وما كدتُ أبدأُ..
لم تَتَلقَّ القبيلةُ بُشرايَ بالعشب والماء،

وأما مَنْ أُوتيَ وعْدَه كَظْماً وألقيَ منه مكاناً
ضيِّقاً مُقْرَناً فسوف تصلصلُ مقاودُه ويصلَّى
ندماً يفري وحزناً سعيراً وثُبوراً..

..وهم يسْتقرِئون الرملَ يخُطّون ويمحُون ولوْ
يجدون ملجأً أو مغاراتٍ أو مُدَّخَلاً لَوَلَّوْا إليه وقد
استيأسوا يتضَعْضَعون،
فمن يفتديني بصرخةٍ مُورقَةٍ أو عشبةِ حلمٍ تَخْضَرُّ في
مراحم التأويل أو غيمةٍ وَدَقٍ مبشِّرٍ!
هلك الطالبُ والمطلوبْ..

وقلتُ: احتملْ غُمَّةَ البرمكيّين، ليس لها دونَ

شعبِ الجزيرة كاشفةُ ..فجأةً سوف يعلو

غبارُ الجزيرة أَلويةً ..

قد تكون دماً هامةً يتأَجَّلُ إرواؤها قد

تكون بأفواههم صرخةُ الفتحِ ..

قلتُ: احتملْ غُمَّةَ البرمكيّين ..قد ثَقُلَتْ في

يديْكَ ورجليكَ أصفادُهم وهمو

رَغَبٌ طامعٌ يتحشَّدهُم ..فاحتملْ ما

ترى من عصاميّةٍ للتواطؤٍ، من

صلفِ الادِّعاءِ المداهِن ..

قلتُ احتملْ نعمةً تتقطَّر من أوْجُهِ البرمكيين عافيةً

وامتلاءَ دمٍ وامتلاكاً لظهر البسيطةِ،

فَلْتَحتملْ ما ترى من رخاوتهم

وتخلُّعهم باكتمالِ الخنوثةِ والكبرياء

فذلك بهوُ نواويسِهم وهو غربتُكَ

المستفيضةُ بالروعِ أسرُكَ في الظمأ الحجريِّ

وفيضُ الهواجسِ عضُّ القيودِ على معصميكَ ورجليكَ ..

همهمةٌ للحديد وجائشةٌ للمُحبَّك من زَرَدِ الجند ..

ولَّتْ غواشي التقلُّبِ في المشهدِ الوحْشِ ..

وانشقَّ من فَلَقِ الصبحِ وجهُكِ يدنو

ويدنو كبارقةِ الغيمِ في صحراء القبيلة ..

هذا إذنْ قمرُ الماءِ يرسفُ في مرمر البرمكين!

واصطَفَّ خلقٌ كثيرٌ ..

فلما اشتبكنا دماً وافتديتِ الأسيرَ بهزَّةِ رأسٍ

٤٣

وأوسعت لي من مقامي وتَوَّجتني باجتلائك
عريانةً وتكسَّرت بين ذهولي وخوفي اقتربتُ ابتعدتُ فقد
سطعَ القَسَمُ الصعبُ من ليل أسجاعه امتدَّ بيني
وبينك أفْقُ المضارب وارتفعت خيمةُ الشَّعر في
المحْل وانعقدتْ غيمةٌ من جراد تشظَّى
تكَشَّفَ وشْيُ الزرابيِّ وانحسرت متفتِّرةً رجفةُ
الفيضان الحريريِّ عن حاصبٍ من سماءٍ تَهَدَّمُ..
أهلَّة فضِّيَّةٌ لامعةٌ من صوت الخبَب قد
سلكتْها طرفاً بطرف حوافر المهرة،
يتراجعُ صداها إلى الوراء ولا يتلاشى،
سلسلةٌ ممتدةٌ هي، تربطُ آخرَ الخطى بأول
الطريق وشهقات الوداع المسجوع وهمهمة
العرّافين وأشكال الكتابة في الرمل ونقوش
التَّحاريق المشجَّرة بالظمأ ورخاوة الموت المعرِّش
بالرماد وشظايا الشمس وصواعق الغرابيب
المنقَضَّة على الجيف
فكيف والصوتُ والصدى حَلَقٌ متداخلٌ يعلو
ويعلو حتى لَيَنْبُعُ من
ضَرَبات القلب ورعدة الجسد الذي يُطوى ويُبسطُ
من رَهَبٍ واشتهاءٍ..فكيفَ..
وهل هودجٌ قمرُ مرمرٌ؟

١٩٧٩

٣- فصلُ المبتدأ المؤخَّر

استفاقَ السيدُ بغتةَ الرؤية في نفسه وفي الآفاق.
قال أفليستْ الأرضُ واسعةً والبلادُ مسرىً ومَقيل!
فخرج من الدمع ولبسَ إحرامَ الجماعة،
وتمنطق بوعي دمه وشهوة الشهادة وقوة
الفطرة العارية من كل كسبٍ واستباق
تلك ولادةٌ يعرف طعمَ زنجبيلها ونكهةً
قهوتها وسليقةَ الأحاديثِ المرسلة
..تلك سليقةُ البشرى:

جموعُ أعينٍ شاخصةٌ
وموجٌ يعلوه موجٌ هو الهاجسُ المنتشر.
صخبٌ واصطفاقُ راياتٍ ورغوةٌ من بهجة
الألوان هو النبأُ العظيمُ المتفلِّتُ من
حدود الكلام وشبكة الصياغة الفاصلة.

قالت له صاحبتُه: عَمَّ يتساءلون!
قال: «لقد مكَرَ الذين من قَبْلِهم فأتى اللهُ
بنيانَهم من القواعد فخَرَّ عليهم السقفُ
من فوقهم وأتاهم العذابُ من حيثُ لا يشعرون»
قالت: لا تحزنْ..أفليست الأرضُ واسعةً!
قال: فليسقطْ ما استعلوا به وملكوا الأرضَ
وليدمدمْ عليهم غضبُ الشعبِ بما أجرموا
قالت: عَذَّبَكَ صوتُ آبائكَ فاسمعْ لهم سَمْعَ الطاعة
وإنهم لرادّوك إلى معادٍ هو طعمُ القهوة
ونكهةُ الهيلِ وشميمُ الحطب في نار القبيلة

فَأحكمْ عقدةَ الكلمة وامتلىءْ بالمجاز
قال: فإنْ لم تفضْ بيَ الأرضُ خرجتُ عليها
ورفعتُ من خواتلِ المجازِ ما يعرفني به
أصحابي وأعرفهم
فإذا جاء الوقتُ امتلأتْ بنا الشِّعابُ.
قالت: وهذا هو ينتصفُ الليلُ
فهل مُتَبِّرٌ أنتَ ما أحكموا من كيدٍ مهما تكن
الظلمةُ فولاذاً صرحاً ممرداً أو
بريقَ سيفٍ مُشْرَعٍ من الأقاصي له
مُكاءٌ وتصدية!
«لو كان عَرَضاً قريباً وسفَراً قاصداً لاتّبعوك»

١

قلت: يا قمرَ الماءِ..بيني وبينك عُقدةُ عشقٍ
تشدُّ عُراها سحابة

تُنَقِّلُ أخفافَها من دمي للفضاء وتُعلي
مقامَك بين العشيرة في آخر الأرض.
للأمهاتِ العجائزَ وَشمُ الأهلَّة والطيرِ،
أقراطُهنَّ دمٌ صدِئٌ يتقطَّر دمعُ تُؤرْجِحُ جوهرَه في
اشتعالِ الضفائر بالشيب غابرةٌ من بروق اللواقحِ.
هذا أنا وانفراطك بين يديَّ ممالكُ من
شهوةٍ وارتباكٍ، سريرُك مُتَّقِدٌ بالعروش الخبيئةِ
والليلُ جمرُ المجرّاتِ والحلمِ،
قلتُ القراءةُ في الرمل والضَّربُ في
كلماتِ الحصى والرياحِ مطارَدَةٌ ليس
تتركني في استتاري بمجد الغواية والعشقِ..
يَصّاعدُ الشِّعرُ بين عظامي غزالةَ شوكٍ
تراكَضُ ركْضَ الصدى في البوادي وتنزف ذاكرتي:

«هوايَ مع الركْبِ اليمانين مُصْعِدُ
جَنيبٌ وجثماني بمكةَ موثَقُ
عجبتُ لِسراها وأنّى تخلَّصَتْ
إليَّ وبابُ السجن دوني مغلقُ
ألَمَّتْ فحيَّتْ ثم قامت فودَّعتْ
فلما تَوَلَّتْ كادت الروحُ تزْهَقُ
فلا تحسبي أني تخشَّعْتُ بعدكم
لشيءٍ ولا أني من الموت أفْرَقُ
ولا أنَّ نفسي يزْدهيها وعيدُهم
ولا أنني بالمشي في القيد أخْرَقُ
ولكنْ عَرَتْني من هواك صبابةٌ
كما كنتُ ألقى منك إذ أنا مُطْلَقُ»

تأوَّلتُ رؤيايَ، هذا الجنونُ الفقيرُ المكدَّسُ بالعشق

والملْك والذهب الدمويِّ ينابذُني جسداً بالمجازات

روحاً بوهج الخلاخيل أسورَةً بالقيود تَعَضُّ على

معصميَّ، جنونٌ فقيرْ

تأوَّلته، وتكذَّبتُ رَميَ الحصى والكتاباتِ في الرمل

فلْينظروا:

ملْكةٌ أمةٌ في حبائل عبد أميرْ

وحوتُ من المرمر الأرجوانيِّ يحملُ فوق

تعاريقه وزعانفه الذهبية بحراً رُخاءً

وزورقَ آنية فضةٍ يتهادى على الماء،

بين الفضا والغيوم السرير

تَخَوَّفتُ أن يعرفوني، تكذَّبتُ ما يكتبون على

الرمل، مَوَّهْتُ ما يقرأون

وأقبلتُ في زُخرُف العشق

هيأتُ من جسدي مثلما يفعلُ الميتون:

حُنوطٌ وطيبٌ يؤخِّر ما يفضحُ الموتَ،

أبهةٌ من هُوَيْنى وخَطْوٍ ثقيلٍ، وأقمطةٌ من

شيات، وباذخةً كفنٌ من حرير

وأنت تألَّفْتني بوعود القيامةِ من جسدينا ومن

جسد الوقت، قلَّبْتني بين حالين:

حالٍ هي العشقُ في مرمر الملكوت،

وحالٍ هي المجدُ في ملكوت الجنون الفقير..

٣

–: أهذا هو العَوْدُ على البدء؟

–: أجَلْ هو العَوْدُ على البدء.

–: كيف وقد أصبحتَ اسماً من أسماء الذاكرة
ولأشجاركَ خشبٌ في المواقد ورائحةٌ في
الوليمة التي تَتَّسعُ لوافدين يتزاحمون!

–: في البدء كنتُ – بين أمي وأبي – اسماً من
أسماء الحلم وطقساً من طقوس الماء المشمولة
بغَبَشِ الفجر وأباريقِ الفخّار واللُّبانِ المرِّ
وبقايا الحنّاء على الكعبين
وكانت قصارُ السُّوَرِ تنعقدُ خيمةً على
استئنافات الصبِّا وإيقاعاتِ الضحى والليل
إذا سجى

هو العَوْدُ على البدء
الليلُ والنهارُ بوابتان على طريق المملكة
أبي عن يميني وأمي عن شمالي والبلادُ تخلع
لهجةَ الطفولة وتعلو منصّةً لكلام الوعد والوعيد
وتمتدُّ حصيرةً للخوف والجوع ومخدّةً للكوابيسِ
والماءُ جمرةُ التذكر الموقَدَة
أنفخ فيها وأنظر ما وراء زخرف الصخر
ومرمر المجازات
لأشهدَ كيف يكون مجدُ الينابيعِ المنتفضة.

عقدةٌ من ضفائرك انفرطتْ بين كفيَّ

خامرني من عصافير حنّائها وروائحها طائفٌ من

دوارٍ،

وزلزلةٌ لم تَكَد تعتريني حتى رأيتُ سهيلاً

يلامحني من ذؤاباتها،

والثريّا المدلاةُ فوق السريرِ تُؤَرْجِحها سنةٌ من نعاسٍ.

ومرت سحابة

تحلُّ عُراها وتفتح أزرارَها، استترت في

زجاج السماوات وانكشفتْ ومضةً ومضةً وهي

تخْصف تاجاً من السعف الغضِّ،

بين يدَيْها تهبُّ الرمالُ المضيئةُ والطيرُ عاصفةً

والمياهُ تصلصل بين السماوات صلصلةً تَتَقَبَّبُ

ناشرةً في الفضاء البعيد جناحين من ظلمة الفيضان،

فهل ناقةٌ هَدَرَتْ فانتبهنا على

مرمر القصر يخلعُ أقدامَه من مواطئها،

القصرُ يرفعُ مرساتَه ويلملمُ خُطوتَه الحجريّةَ

من مَقلع الأرض يرفعُ أعمدةً من

دخانٍ وأتربة تتموَّجُ في الريح؟

هل ناقةٌ هدرتْ فالرِّواقُ المهدَّمُ يرجفُ

بالماءِ يزَّلزلُ الهودجُ الملكيُّ وتهوي

السلاسلُ فالأرضُ مفتوحةٌ لجةً؟

أم تأوَّلتُ رؤيايَ فاتقدتْ من

سريرك غاشيةٌ من جنون المجازات!

١٩٨٠/١٩٧٩/١٩٧٥

فَرَحٌ بالهواء

هي المرةُ الواحدة
إلى أوَّل البدءِ أو آخرِ المنتهى، ينتهي كلُّ شيءٍ:
هما جسدان على بقعةِ الدمِ: قَتْلٌ هو السحرُ
مقتولةٌ وقتيلٌ
فأيهما سدَّدَ النصلَ
أيهما ابتدرَ الفعلَ والإنفعالَ؟

هي الطعنةُ الواحدة
فأيُّهما أشْعلتْه من الجمرة الموقدة
قبلةٌ تتلصَّصُ حتى امتزاج الدم العنفوانيِّ
أو صرخةُ النشوة المتواشجةُ الآه بالموت؟
أيهما تتشقَّقُ فيه الينابيعُ.. هَذا الأبُ
المتواترُ بين الضلوع
أم الرحمةُ المستكنَّةُ في الرحم الواعدة؟
وهذا المؤجَّلُ حتى إذا انقصفَ العمرُ،
حتى إذا انحسرَ الوهمُ..
لا جسدُ المرأة المجهدة
يجيبُ الدمَ المتوقِّدَ أجوبةَ النار
أو يرحم العطشَ المتشعِّعَ في الكأس بالماءِ
والطينَ بالحلمِ

والنومَ بالطيران إلى الشمسِ
واللقمةَ المستريبةَ في القمح بالشِّعْر
والوطنَ الذائبَ الطعمِ في خَطفةِ الرِّيقِ بالسحرِ،
والجثةَ الهامدة
بآخرِ ما صفَّدتْه الفُجاءةُ في الروح من رقصةِ البرقِ!
هذي هي الطعنةُ الواحدة
تراخَتْ بها لحظةُ الحسْمِ، راوغَها زمنٌ يتطاولُ بالعشقِ
فاستترتْ – والشهودُ يمرون في الحافلات
ويندلقون على حجرِ السعي – لا شاهدُ يتملّى
– من الكحلِ والنمنمات المضيئة
تحت النطاقين والرقصة البدوية –

بارقةَ النصلِ، لا شاهدة
تُعَرِّي الخطى عن سياقِ الصعودِ إلى الموتِ بالعشقِ،
لا تتكشَّفُ وَقْدَ جنونِ المجازاتِ في طينةِ الوجهِ وهي
مُحيَّرةٌ بين صمتٍ بليغٍ وثرثرةٍ تتشظَّى إشاراتُها،

كان صبحُ الشتاءِ المبكرُ يرمي

مناديلَه من رذاذٍ خفيفٍ
ورفرفةِ الغيمِ بين الغصونِ النواعسِ،
كانت بقايا الكرى
تحت ذَرْوٍ من الكحلِ والسهَرِ المتفتِّرِ تومضُ
ومضاً يُتَعْتِعُ منه الخطى فهو سكرانُ يقظانُ،

كان الصباحُ المبلَّلُ بالطَّلِّ والغيمِ
يفتح في وحشةِ الأرضِ والروحِ نافذةً فالسماءُ البعيدةُ
شفّافةٌ والطيورُ الحوائمُ تُبدع أشكالَ بهجتها ونداءاتها ..
تلك كانت صلاةُ الضحى:

اصطفَّ فيضُ الخلائق منتعشاً بالوضوء الجماعيِّ، ثم استوى الخلقُ تحت الفضاء العميق
قياماً تحاذَتْ خطاه وقاماتُه
بين خطين:
بيتٍ جميعٍ هو الأرضُ، حلمٍ جميعٍ هو الأَفْقُ،

عدلُ جميعٌ هي البهجةُ المستثارةُ أَلوانُها في نوافير طيرٍ يُعيدُ ويُبدىءُ نسجَ السماوات والصحو، تكبيرةٌ من دويِّ التنازيل والوحي تعلو بها خضرةُ الحيِّ، سانحةُ القلق المشرئبةُ تحت سطوح الجوامد، إيقاعُ ما يتوجَّعُ من ممكنات التماثيل في الصخر، ما يتَحَلَّبُ من شبق الشِّعْرِ في عُقدة النهد بين التويجات، ما يتهتَّكُ من لذة النضج في الثمر المتهاوي إلى زغب العشب.
يبتلُ وجدُ الخلائق في الركعة الحاشدة بدمع التأويل، يعلو الدعاءُ بما يتنفَّسه الصبحُ والأرضُ،
يعلو دمي في دويِّ التراتيل ماءً مع الماء طيناً مع الطين شكلاً
يئنُ به الصخرُ زخرفةً تتشجَّر في بهجة الطير صمتاً هو الشعرُ والشهقةُ الشاردة
وعيناك من أَرَقِ الكحل والزئبق المتصدِّف صمتٌ بليغٌ وثرثرةٌ تتشظَّى إشاراتُها وأنا الزفْرةُ المحضُ..

–: مِمَّنْ، ومن إين؟

–: لا أرضَ لا وقتَ.. إني اطَّرَحْتُهما من ورائي فلستُ سوى زفرةٍ مِن هيولى سوى قطرةٍ من دمٍ تتشحَّطُ تحت يد الله وهو يقلِّبها ما يشاءُ على

ظمأ يتسعَّرُ أو حسرةٍ عاقدة.

ـ: فكيف ارتوى طميُ وجهكَ بي فهو طميُ بلادي؟
وأي يدٍ
حفَّرتْ في جبينكَ مسطورَ أغنيتي في صِبا العمر أو
بعثرتْ في لوامع شيبتكَ الهمجية
ما ضاق عنه المدى من
خيول الجموحات واستبهمتْه الرؤى البائدة
من العشق والعُرْيِ تحت يد الله؟

ـ: من أي جمرٍ مقيمٍ وعمرٍ هشيمٍ تقيمين هذا الصباحَ
على العرش فاتحةً في صلاة الخليقة واللهُ ينفخ من
روح أسمائه الدهشةَ الراصدة؟

سماءُ المدينة مغسولةٌ تتدلَّى ثُريّا نهارٍ ومشكاة صحوٍ بليل،
تمدُ شوارعُها من مُخَلَّع كاشيِّها وحجارتها خطوةً يتغاوى
بها السعيُ أو خطوةً تتدلَّه فيها البصيرةُ..
تعلو خفيفاً خفيفاً فترجفُ
بين الرؤى والدم المتشتِّت أرضٌ تغاوتْ بنا
فهي تخطو خطانا
وتفتحُ بهو الممالكِ:
سجادةٌ تتقلَّب في متنها رجفةُ الروح، نافورةُ
الطير والورق الغض، وهجُ الظهيرة والقنص، جُرْحُ
وسافيةٌ في الدَّياميم، هَرْجُ الغزالات، خيلٌ وأروقةٌ
للملوك وصمتٌ يحفُ ستائرَ بيت الحريم
وصمتٌ يلفُ المجازَ
المؤدّي إلى قاعة العرشِ

٥٤

كنا انتهينا إلى البهو لا أنا مني ولا أنت منك وقد
أطلق الواسطيُّ نياقَ تصاويره تشرب الماءَ من
راحتيكِ وتبدأ ترجيعها بالحنين المزلزلِ

-: هل هذه الرشفةُ الباردة
تردُّ قطيع النياق إلى الواسطيِّ - المعمم بالشمس -
حلماً وآصرةً بين فرشاته والسماوات؟
هل رشفةٌ تستعيدُ قطيعَ المواويلِ من ظمأً من الأربعينَ؟

-: استمعْ..أنتَ ضيفٌ على رحمة الغيم..فاستنْزل
الريحَ واصمتْ..فليس يُلقّى من الغيم رحمتَه غيرَ مَن
يبدعُ الصمتَ والإنتظارَ..استمعْ..إن ريحاً ترتِّلُ
من ورْدِ أحوالها همهمات الولادات في الإرث طقسَ
ارتواءِ الخليقة بين السماوات والأرض بالرهبة الخالدة
أمام انفساح الفضاءات والجمر في قلب من
يبدعون انتظاراتهم فَيُلَقَّوْنَ من مدَدِ السمعِ
كيف تخوض الخليقةُ أوجاعَ
بهجتها ومخاضاتها .
إنه العشقُ في مصحف الكون وهو
القصيدةُ في حمأ الخلق..فاسمعْ..

تقَضَّى من الصمت ليلٌ طويلٌ
ألقَى به من عطايا الضيافة بشرايَ
سيدتي: هل دمي في الدوارق أم شالُكِ المزْدَهي
بالسماوات والأرضِ يمتدُّ للمائدة
فيأتي رعاياكِ من كل زوجين فالأرضُ مُحْضَرَةٌ في احتفالية
العشق والوحي!

ذَوَّبني الدمعُ طمياً من الطمي

-: أنتَ البلادُ التي اختمرتْ في الرؤى والتي
لم يلدني سواها

-: وأنت البلادُ التي عقدتْني بأرحامها مُضْغَةً، ثم أحْيَيْتِ
مني الخليقةَ فانفجرتْ دهشةً من صباها

-: دمُ في دمٍ أم زلازلُ ماءٍ تدمدمُ
في طبقات التذكر والحلم؟
رجْعُ نياقٍ من الظمأ المتشقِّق أم صرخةٌ تتململ في
دارس العمر بين الطلولِ؟

-: أنا وتدُ السَّنْط..كانت خيامُ العشيرة تبلى
ويكنسها العصفُ واحدةً واحدة
وأبقى أُلملمُ في قامتي ما ترجِّعه الريحُ من
ذكريات العقائل والخيل

-: شالي خباءٌ وخيمةُ شَعْرٍ مرفرفةٌ في يديكَ.

-: وأنتِ بلادُ موطَّأةُ الماء والعشب

-: أنتَ سماءُ السكينة، أنتَ المغني المشرَّدُ
ما بين قطعان حبي..

انقضتْ ليلةٌ من كلام التأويل والصمت
والفجرُ ينشر غُبشتَه طاوياً أربعين بساطاً – هي العمرُ –

من دمٍ وبقايا رمادِ المواقدِ حتى انكشفْتُ وحيداً
وأطلَلتُ..كانت براري العشيرة موحشةً..وأنا
وتدُ السَّنْط تحت سماواتها أتكشَّفُ هودَجَ عشقٍ
يهلُّ وخيمةَ شَعَرٍ وباديةٍ يتقطَّر فيها من العشب
جَمْرُ البراعمِ..

قلتُ: اسمعي..إن قطعانَ حبِّكِ طالعةٌ في
ندى الفجر ثاغيةً والمغني يلملم إيقاعَ مواله
من خطى الريح..

قالت: له ليلةٌ سوف ينسى بها ما رأى..فاستمعْ..إن
شمساً تَخَلَّلُ من سعف النخل
تمسحُ خلف الزجاج الستائرَ..
موعدُنا صمتُ ليلٍ تُلَقَّى به خَطْفَةَ الروح بين
السماوات والأرض والشهقة الموصدة..

يغني المغني..وشهقةُ موّاله انشرختْ نَوْحَ باكيةٍ
وانخطافَ صَباً جرَّرَتْ ذيلَها في خزامى العشيرة
واستنطقتْ جلَّنارَ الضفائرِ والحبقِ المتفتحَ
في مفْرق الشَعْرِ،
وابتردتْ في اندلاع المروج العفيَّة بالخضرة الماردة
يغني أم الحلمُ أم أرضُ مجدٍ من الدم والفقرِ
أم صبوةٌ من سماءٍ تَتَنَزَّلُ؟
فجرٌ يشعشع في لهفة القلب أم شبقٌ
تستضيءُ التواريخُ تحت ارتباكاته أم دمٌ
يتشوَّفُ وهْجَ مناراته؟
غربةٌ أم هو العطشُ الحجريُّ المفتَّتُ بيداً من الرملِ

تنأى امتداداتُها أم ملاعبُ جنٍّ ووحشٍ تخطُّ
الرياحُ مساراتها ومواجعَها أم يغني المغني؟

أنا وتد السنط.. في قامتي كبرياء الترقُّب.. في جسدي
كبرياءُ الملوك الذين يُلقَّوْنَ في جريان السلالة
آياتِ عرقِهمو بين صمتِ رمادٍ وريحٍ مبشِّرةٍ..
في جلالِ اصطفائك إياي كانت بوادي العشيرة
تعلو إلى ساطع الحلم، قطعانُك انتشرتْ والمواويل في
مطلق الريح والصمتِ مرسلةٌ،

قلتُ: من أين، أيّان مُتَّجَهُ الخطو، أيَّةُ تفعيلةٍ والدة
ستشرخ صوتي وتفتح في فيضان الرؤى وكثافة إيقاعها
طلعةَ الرجعِ والصَّدْع؟

ليلَتئذْ كنتِ توريةً شفّ إيحاؤها عن طلاسم
مجد قديم من العشق أُنسيتُه وبلادٍ وأعمدة من
رخامٍ ورملٍ وأدعيةٍ كنتِ مكنونةً في اشتهائي
وطالعةً من قواريرِ عطرٍ تعتَّق في أزل الشرق
كانت كمائمُ وردِ حريرٍ تشفُّ وتبرُقُ منها
كنوزُ السلائبِ من أرق المصطفين
يدُ رعدتي واشتهائي يدُ ومجازُ العشيرة تسقط
عنه الغلائلُ تشرق لي من كنوز السلائب جوهرةً وامضة
أحلُّ حريرَ طلاسمك البكْر ألتفُّ في سحرها أتلقَّط
منها عطايا غرائبها طَيَّةً طيةً.. والإشاراتُ
شفَّتْ مجازاتها، أخذتني بروقُ من الوجد والخوف،
وانقدحتْ آهةٌ تتنزَّلُ بالدهشة الراعدة
وكفاكِ من رحمة الغيم تستبدلان دماً بدمٍ

وسماءً بأخرى، تخطان فوق جبينيَ أرضاً هي
المحْوُ للعمر والطلعُ في نخلة للبدايات والفجر
– كان الحنان ندى يتقطّر في طينتي – كان دفءُ
يديك يلملمُ ما بعثرتْه ندوبُ الولادة
والوَحَم المتكدِّس من
أمهاتي القديمات، ينثر ما يتفكَّكُ من خَرَز الظَّهر،
يُوقدُ في العظم واللحم أخيلةَ الطيران الطليق..
أخفُّ تخفِّين، لا أنت منكِ ولا أنا مني،
استوينا دماً واحداً..

–: ميتُ واحدُ كيف ينقسم الموتُ فيه إلى جثتين؟

–: هي الجثةُ الواحدة

–: فكيف إذا اقتتل الأهلُ كي يملأوا حفرتين ترابين كانا
تراباً يكوِّمه العشقُ في ركعة الوجد؟

–: ليِّنةٌ خطوة الطين في الطين: تلْتمُّ من
تحتنا الأرضُ سجادةً، يرتمي في التراب الترابُ وفي
سجدة العشق لا ساجدٌ يتكشَّفُ في دمه عن
دمٍ تتجلى به الساجدة
دمُ واحدٌ يتشحَّط في ظلمة الأرض تحت يد الله،
ثمَّ تقلّبه في يد القدرة الريحُ، يعلو خفيفاً
ويأخذ مسراه في ساطعٍ من معارجَ الغامضة
وسيعاً كما تقتضي قامةُ الكون، أضيقَ من
شهقة الروح في الروحِ.
بين السماوات والأرض ريحٌ تغاوتْ بنا فهي

تخطو خطانا ونخطو خطاها،
الفضاءات رقْصُ غواياتنا..فالمآذنُ أوتادُ خيمتنا
والقبابُ ارتخاءُ يدينا، الصحارى
مخدَّةُ قيلولةٍ والمعابدُ شكلُ أصابعنا في
اشتباكاتها لحظة الحلم..
نحن القميصُ المرقَّط بالأنجم المزهرات وبالشجر الرطب
والدور، نحن الخلاءُ المقدَّرُ بين المجرَّات
والنغمُ المنتشي في مسير الكواكب
نحن انفجار الحضارات في اللغة البكر
أولنا الزفرةُ المحضُ
آخرُنا محضُ تفعيلةٍ والدة..

١٩٨٨/٢/١٢